The Evolving Story of
CEDARMORE

Alfred Grimwade

authorHOUSE®

AuthorHouse™ UK Ltd.
500 Avebury Boulevard
Central Milton Keynes, MK9 2BE
www.authorhouse.co.uk
Phone: 08001974150

First published by AuthorHouse 10/6/2009

ISBN: 978-1-4490-0964-9 (sc)

This book is printed on acid-free paper.

This book is dedicated to
Brian Cooper, Ron Dungate and Reg Shore,
esteemed friends and very special colleagues in the work of
Cedarmore
over many years

Contents

FOREWORD

Donald Cranefield

Forty years ago, faith like the proverbial mustard seed planted Cedarmore. How it grew into a mighty tree in which, over the years, no less than 400 'little birds' have nested safely in its branches is the remarkable story told here by Alfred Grimwade. It is a story which from the outset to the present day is a tapestry of that mustard seed faith, moving many mountains, outstanding professional competence and, above all, sheer hard work. In recent years much of the industry required in the running of Cedarmore has been supplied by those with the time and energy available in their retirement years. In those early demanding years, those who devoted their energies and expertise were in the prime of their lives, engaged in responsible business practice. It is a commitment that few in their position would so willingly accept today.

My introduction to Cedarmore was five long years after that first meeting in George and Margaret Duke's home in Cedar Road, but just six months following the joyful opening of Cedarmore Court. I can remember now the enthusiasm for the new venture, the glowing pride in a great achievement and a deep desire and commitment to make it work to the glory of God. Following those balmy days of a Cedarmore Springtime it seemed to me that the venture never stood still. One stone laying was followed by the next. In the story as told by Alfred most chapters conclude by encouraging us to read the next. Therein would seem to lie the spirit of Cedarmore, never resting on past achievement but always moving forward to meet new challenges and changing needs of the times.

Although much of the original vision and the subsequent pursuing of new ventures may be attributable to Alfred himself, this story is the testimony to so many who have given their time, competence and energy without counting the cost. They have done this freely and willingly to the glory of God and the serving of those who in the frail evening of their days need a home to live in, someone to care for them and the warmth of companionship to comfort them. Cedarmore for forty years has done all that. Those of us who know it best pray that it may go on doing it for a long time yet.

(Rev Donald Cranefield was minister of Bromley Baptist Church from 1973 to 1990)

FOREWORD

Sir Roger Sims

Over my 23 years as the local MP I got to know all the sheltered housing schemes and residential homes in my constituency. Some were run by the local authority, some by commercial concerns and charitable bodies and some by the various newly emerging housing associations. Each had its own particular style and characteristics. But, for me Cedarmore and Southmore were notable for the relaxed yet efficient manner in which these sheltered homes were run and the obvious caring atmosphere within them. And the more I learned about Cedarmore Housing Association over subsequent years the more impressed I became. A handful of men from a local church had voluntarily pooled their skills and devoted much of their time to planning and building first one then another well designed sheltered housing scheme and to creating caring and supportive communities within them. This seemed to me a very real demonstration of putting Christian principles into practice – but it did not end there. After the sheltered housing had been running for a time Cedarmore recognised the need for a care home – so they built one. Then they realised that some of the residents who had developed dementia needed a separate unit – so they built one. And thus Cedarmore continued to expand.

How all this was planned and achieved is related in these pages and shows what can be done by a small forward looking group of committed volunteers, enthused by their faith. It is an inspiring account. The final chapters contain some thoughtful comments on the way in which housing associations have developed and the extent of State support for the elderly. I feel that they merit careful consideration – not least by the present generations of politicians!

Meanwhile, Cedarmore stands as an endeavour of which the original founders, not least the author, can be proud. And it is one for which many elderly people thank them and thank God and will do so for many years to come.

(Sir Roger Sims was Member of Parliament for Chislehurst from 1974 until he retired in 1997)

INTRODUCTION

This book has been written in response to the feeling expressed by a number of people that there should be some written record of the development of the work of Cedarmore Housing Association and an account of how its various schemes came into being. It was suggested to me that as I appeared to be the only surviving founder member of the organisation and the only person still alive who has had the privilege of being involved at the beginning of all of those schemes that I was the person who should produce this. I did not take the suggestion very seriously at first; having never written a book before and I doubted if I should find the time. During the early part of 2008, however, a strong feeling came over me that the Cedarmore story had to be told so that present and future residents and staff and those who support the work may be aware of the origins of the Association and its various schemes and of the objectives and behind them. It seemed important, also, to relate how a small group of like-minded people working together and supported by their churches were able to meet particular needs in their community and how God blessed their work.

Having concluded that a book of some kind had to be written and that I should probably have to attempt the task, I decided that I had better try to do so as soon as possible whilst my memory of the events and of the various people involved is still fairly clear. It was my privilege to be on the management committee of Cedarmore from its beginnings in 1968 until 2003 and it has been an important part of my life for many years. I cannot claim, therefore, to have an unbiased view as to the value of its work and its achievements! However, I have tried to give a fair and honest account of the various events as I recall them and some insight into the decisions leading up to them. It has seemed essential, too, to refer to some of the many people involved. Fortunately in a way, I have always been somewhat of a hoarder and have been able to retrieve from the filing cabinet in my garage copies of the minutes of all management committee meetings from January 1969 onwards, as well as copies of many subcommittee meetings. These have been a great help in refreshing my memory of those events and of the decisions and discussions about them. I confess to some pleasant nostalgia as I recalled some of the events and remembered some of the fine people who shared in those discussions. The exercise has brought warm memories, too, of some of the wonderful people who moved into one or other of the Cedarmore schemes and spent the last few years or months of their lives there.

The limitations of this narrative will soon be obvious to most readers. Although over the years I have spent much time drafting reports, writing correspondence, etc I have never found it easy to find the right words to describe situations or issues. Like many accountants, I have tended to do better with figures than with words. A wide useable vocabulary has never been one of my strong points and, as one gets older, that weakness persists. If that shortcoming irritates some readers, I hope they will understand when they realise that almost all of it has been written in my 87th year - another reason perhaps why relating this story should not be delayed any longer!

Readers will discover that, in writing this narrative, I have been unable to refrain from expressing an opinion on one or two issues as they have arisen. Those who know me well will not be surprised by this! However, I should like to make it clear that those views are entirely my own and are not necessarily shared by others who have worked with me in Cedarmore work or by present members of its management committee. Although few of the issues discussed are very controversial, I strongly suspect that one or two may see the issue or interpret events slightly differently. So far as I am aware, the book will not have been seen by any of the present management committee members before its publication. Although I believe they will welcome it and, hopefully, may find it useful occasionally, they can disclaim entirely any responsibility for it. That responsibility is entirely my own!

I am grateful to a number of people who have helped me put this book together.

Amongst these are my longstanding friends, Norman and Mary Tinker, who have read through the whole of the narrative and given me their comments upon it. Norman was one of my colleagues in those early days when the Cedarmore idea was first discussed at the Bromley Baptist Church Men's Fellowship. Although he never came on to any Cedarmore committee, he strongly supported the original proposal and he and Mary have been quiet supporters of the work in so many ways over the whole time since then. I am grateful, too, to Rev Donald Cranefield and Sir Roger Sims for taking the trouble to peruse the book and write forewords to it. As the narrative will reveal, both took a keen interest in the work of Cedarmore for many years and this was a great encouragement to us. Once again, Derek Waller has shown his interest in the work of Cedarmore by using his outstanding artistic skills to produce the cover for this book and I am very grateful to him for this.

I should like to mention one or two others who have helped me in very practical ways. Firstly, the two Mike's - Mike Windsor, and my son-in-law, Mike Ross; who only a few years ago, against all the odds, set me on the road of using a personal computer. Without this and its amazing word processor facility, I should not have got far with my old typewriter. Secondly, my daughters, Angela and Heather, who have guided me in electronic communication and on bringing my writings together and storing them safely - advice which was a great help to me after, for some unknown reason, ten pages which I had written had mysteriously disappeared from the screen. . Finally, I must pay special tribute to my wife Eleanor for her strong support and for her great patience in tolerating so much of my spare time in this past year being pre-occupied with this task.

Whatever use may be made of this narrative - and that may well turn out not to be very much - I do hope some will derive pleasure from reading it. To a few it may bring back memories of events and people they have known in the Bromley area during the latter part of the 20th century. To others who have been involved in similar voluntary work, it may strike a chord as they recall similar challenges and tensions in their own deliberations. I dare to hope, too, that there may be those of a younger generation who aspire to service and have a desire to express their Christian faith in some practical way for the benefit of others less advantaged than themselves, who may just be encouraged by this story. If it does all or any of this, the effort will have been worthwhile.

PART I
EARLY DAYS

Chapter 1
Vision and Origin

So often in the realm of social, economic and indeed religious activity it is possible to look at the origin of a work and see that it blended in with a general pattern or trend amongst like-minded people at the time, perhaps without those involved being aware of it. This is certainly true of Cedarmore. A change of thinking, which perhaps was a feature of the sixties in society generally, was taking place also in Church life and in the attitude of Christian communities towards social needs in society. The Keele Conference in 1964 had reawakened in many Evangelicals in Britain the conviction that, in addition to evangelism, faith needed to be expressed in practical service and concern for the underprivileged. Churches were beginning to respond to this in various ways. One social need which was highlighted at that time was the acute housing shortage - highlighted by the *Kathy Come Home* film shown on television - and unsatisfactory housing provision for older people. British Council of Churches responded by forming the British Churches Housing Trust, largely to assist and encourage churches to develop housing schemes. Many of the well known church housing associations had their origins around that time, including the Baptist Housing Association (originally the Baptist Men's Movement Housing Association). Bromley Council of Churches had responded by supporting the formation of Burnt Ash Housing Association and its development of St Andrew's House, a small sheltered housing scheme in Burnt Ash Lane which still functions to-day.

Richard Carr-Gomm, a retired Guards officer who had been greatly influenced during the Billy Graham Harringay Crusade, had opened his first small home for older people in Abbeyfield Road Bermondsey and by 1969 there were a number of Abbeyfield Society houses for older people in various parts of the country supported by local church groups.

Bromley Baptist Church (known to many as 'Park Road') had a thriving Men's Fellowship, a group of twenty or more men who would meet fortnightly on a Friday evening. It was perhaps not surprising then that when they began to consider whether they could compliment their normal activity with some form of practical service, the idea of housing to meet the needs of older people soon came to mind. The idea was encouraged by a letter from the minister at the time, Godfrey Robinson, enquiring as to whether the men could do something to help a number of elderly people in the Church congregation who were coping inadequately in inappropriate accommodation. Examples of successful projects at other churches were discovered, particularly at Haven Green Ealing and College Road Harrow and men involved in those schemes came over to Bromley to tell us their stories. A special meeting to consider the possibility of a similar project in Bromley was held on13 February 1968 and men's groups in other local Baptist Churches were invited to share in the discussion. In the event Crofton Baptist Church was the only other church to be represented at that meeting - by Norman Foy. However, his presence was crucial and marked the beginning of the major involvement of the Crofton Church in the work of Cedarmore which has continued right up to the present time.

That meeting was chaired by George Duke, the Men's Group chairman, and, like several subsequent meetings, was held at his house in Cedar Road, a turning off Widmore Road in Bromley - the address from which the name 'Cedarmore' was later derived. It viewed the idea positively and decided to set up a steering committee to examine the issues involved and the practicability of the Group carrying through a project of this kind. The four men on the steering committee were Norman Burke, Dewi Jenkins, Jim Drummond and the writer. Of those four, only Norman had had any practical experience of housing development and his knowledge and contacts proved of great value. Various enquiries and consultations were held, including meetings with the Bromley Town Clerk, British Churches Housing Trust and others and a report on the Committee's findings was submitted to a special

Men's Groups meeting at Bromley Baptist Church on 17 September 1968. By that time two or three other Baptist churches men's groups had shown an interest, including Elm Road Beckenham and Elmstead Lane Chislehurst. The report concluded positively, though cautiously, as follows:

Although such a scheme would entail considerable effort and make no little demand on the resources of service available, the Committee are of the view that such a scheme would not be outside the scope of our Men's Groups in the Borough, supplemented by help from others within our churches. The facilities available and the enormous need existing would seem to make this a challenge which can be met and which could provide a very adequate return by way of relieving some of the care and easing some of the burdens which come so often in the eventide of life .

Looking back now after 40 years, few would quarrel with the prediction in the first line of the above or with the prediction as to the 'return' envisaged (even if the language is a little archaic!).

Those who met on 17 September enthusiastically accepted the challenge of the Report and positive steps towards forming a housing association started to be taken. One of the first requirements was to find a few more experienced people willing to join in the work and take a seat on the Management Committee of the new association. Surprisingly this did not prove too difficult for most of those approached willingly shared in the challenge. They included three Park Road deacons - Cecil Lloyd, a solicitor and senior partner at Wellers, Bernard Cook, a building surveyor and Graham Ratcliff, a local Bank manager - and Marion Wilmshurst, a nurse who was at that time Matron of the Dunoran Nursing Home, then part of Bermondsey and Brook Lane Medical Mission, and Chris Bull, an accountant from Elm Road Church Beckenham.

Not surprisingly, some time was spent agreeing a name for the new body. The name Bromley Baptist Housing Association was considered but a less denominational name was felt to be more appropriate and when someone suggested 'Cedarmore' for the reasons referred to above, this was happily settled on.

With the encouraging prospect of a team of this strength working together on the project, the first task then was to get a housing association formally established so that there would be a legal entity to acquire and develop any property or site which became available. Here the contacts already established with British Churches Housing Trust (Richard Best, now Lord Best, was then its Housing Adviser!) and the National Federation of Housing Associations (Valerie Clarke) proved invaluable The NFHA Model Rules for a charitable housing association were with their help quickly adapted to our situation. In early December an application for registration under the Industrial and Provident Societies Act 1965 was signed by the seven people who were to be its first members and submitted to the Registrar of Friendly Societies who issued their formal confirmation of registration on 11 December 1968. The Housing Corporation did not exist at that time but steps were taken to register the Association as a charity and this was granted formally in June 1969.

The first meeting of the Management Committee was held on 2 January 1969 and the minutes of that meeting make interesting reading. George Duke was appointed the first Chairman of the Association, the writer its Honorary Secretary and Chris Bull, its Honorary Treasurer. Later Ron Smith, an accountant member of Park Road agreed to become Honorary Auditor. So the framework was now complete, the enthusiasm was there and all that was now needed was a project - or, at least, a site on which to develop one. If this was to be God's work, as everyone on that committee wanted it to be, that need would be met - but they were made to wait for while as the next chapter will show.

Chapter 2
Searching for the first Development

Although most people to-day would be familiar with the concept of sheltered housing for older people, this was far from the case in 1969 when there were few schemes in existence which would be so described. In the immediate post war years, a number of schemes for accommodating and caring for older people had been developed by voluntary organisations and local authorities. Most of this was in the form of either a nursing home or a 'Part III' home. The latter was really a residential care home although those living in them were considerably more active than most folk in residential care homes to-day. There was little provision for those older people who did not wish to go into a residential or nursing care situation and could manage in more independent accommodation if there was someone at hand for emergencies and who would give the security and mild supervision which they needed. Abbeyfield houses, with their resident housekeeper, had become one way of responding to this. Purpose built sheltered accommodation in blocks of self-contained flats was a comparatively new concept.

The Steering Committee in its recommendations had shied away from the idea of a residential care home, partly because of the amount of administration likely to be involved, but also because they felt that most of their potential residents would prefer as much independence as possible. However, they were drawn to the idea of sheltered housing which seemed more likely to meet their need. One such scheme had been successfully started by the church at College Road, Harrow and another, nearer at hand at West Wickham, by Beckenham Old People Welfare Association. Both appeared to be working well. The Committee had recommended a small scheme of this kind, as the project which the new organisation should try to develop.

At its first meeting in January 1969, the Management Committee had before it that recommendation and, encouragingly, the newer members of the team had no difficulty in endorsing it. There was no chance of implementing it, however, without a site suitable for development in this way. In addition, they knew they would need professional assistance - architects, quantity surveyors and solicitors - as well, of course, as a sizeable amount of finance. Finding a site took some time but it was surprising how quickly the other factors came together. A local URC member, Ray Wilkins, senior partner in Beard Bennett Wilkins agreed to be the Architect for the new scheme and to advise on the development potential of sites which became available. Eric Bass, a quantity surveyor member of Bromley Baptist Church, offered his firm' services as Quantity Surveyors and Wellers, with whom Cecil Lloyd was associated agreed to act as Solicitors.

The Steering Committee had explored possible sources of finance and had been pleased to discover that long term finance for such a scheme was obtainable from the Local Authority if it met their criteria for housing finance. Norman Burke and the writer had had a helpful meeting with the Bromley 'Town Clerk' at the time, Percy Bunting, and he had encouraged them to apply for such a loan when a suitable scheme was ready.

Looking back at that situation nearly 40 years later when flat development in the Bromley area is still in full swing and developers are finding fresh opportunities in all parts of the Borough, it seems surprising that it was difficult to find a small site suitable for Cedarmore in 1969. But residential development was still tightly controlled and the competition for suitable sites was strong. The patience and faith of the new Committee was to be well tested. They believed that they had a mission to perform and, in the end, their prayers were answered in a way which they could not have anticipated. In spite of feelers being put out in various directions, it was not until May 1971 that they were able to exchange contracts for the purchase of the Chislehurst property which became the site for the first development.

During 1969 and 1970 various properties which might be suitable for development were looked at and discussed in committee. Surprisingly, perhaps, in view of their lack of any track record, the Association was short listed for a site in Beckenham which the Council was offering for development and which went to a larger housing association. It is also amusing to notice from the minutes that one of the properties thought to be coming on to the market at that time was Bromley College - a listed building of considerable historic interest. One's mind boggles at the thought of what would have happened had Cedarmore somehow become involved in the modernisation and management of this!

In June 1970, quite unexpectedly, the Secretary received information from a local Estate Agent that two adjoining properties in Church Lane Chislehurst were on the market for sale as well as an adjoining piece of land. One of the properties was being used as a small private school which was closing and the other as the private residence of the owner. The separate piece of land was being used as a small riding school. The properties were in a highly desirable area, close to Chislehurst Common. The total asking price for the three properties was £35,400 but the owners would accept a lower price if all three were sold together. It was very obvious that the three properties together would make a highly attractive site for a small development if this were allowed in what was then, and still is, a conservation area. We immediately showed interest in acquiring the whole site and received encouraging response from both the owners and the Agents. Ray Wilkins very quickly put together a sketch plan for a suitable flats development on the site. The owners were made aware from the start of our intentions and appeared to warm to the prospect of the site being used in that way. The question, of course, was as to whether, and to what extent, the Council would grant planning consent for such development in a conservation area. The Committee took an optimistic view on this and was able to reach agreement with the owners for their sale of the three properties together for £30,000, conditional upon planning consent which had to be obtained by 30 September.

Although at that time obtaining outline planning consent was a faster process than it has become subsequently, the Committee were clearly naïve or just very optimistic in expecting to receive this in time to meet the 30 September deadline set by the vendors. The Local Authority understandably felt the need to canvas local opinion on such a development and refused the first application on density of development grounds. Consent for a slightly smaller development eventually received planning consent in March 1971. Parallel with the planning approach, application for loan finance was submitted to Bromley Council. This was favourably received but needed a valuation of the site and this was dependant upon the planning consent. Fortunately the District Valuer was able to confirm the value of the site with that planning consent as not less than £30,000 and a Loan Agreement with the Council to cover both the site purchase and its eventual development was signed shortly afterwards.

The vendors were able to be satisfied too, in spite of their earlier 30 September deadline, so that on 6 May 1971, Cedarmore found itself the owners with vacant possession of the three properties in Church Lane, Dunkerrin, Wardley School and the adjoining riding school site, with planning consent for a small sheltered housing development. The site covered the whole area between St Nicholas' Church and The Bulls Head Hotel - between the Church and the Pub as many would subsequently describe it!

Even at the time, onlookers expressed surprise at Cedarmore's having been able to obtain for their first scheme a site in such an attractive location and one for which you might have expected private investors or developers to be clamouring. Looking back, of course, the price of £30,000 seems ridiculously low for such a prime site which if on the market in 2008 might fetch up to £1 million.

How was it then that Cedarmore in its very first property acquisition was able to obtain such a prize? There were several factors which accounted for this. One was the timing - this appears to have been one of those lulls in the private property market which occur from time to time when properties are slow to sell. (Cedarmore was able to take advantage of a similar lull twenty years later when the site for Florence House was acquired.) It coincided too with the decision of the owners to close down Wardley School and the riding school and move out of the area. Redevelopment of the site had perhaps not been seriously considered before we came along and the sympathy of the owners towards our objectives was a helpful factor. Doubtless, too, the quality and experience of the Cedarmore team which by then had been assembled played a part. Having on one committee several people who were carrying wide responsibilities in their own spheres made it easy to recognise that here was a unique opportunity which had to be grasped. And, of course, this was the opportunity for which they had been praying!

Chapter 3
Building Cedarmore Court

The first task was an easy one, though a little painful - to pull down the two old Victorian buildings which had been part of the Church Lane landscape for many years and the stables. Although these properties had their attractions, few doubted that this was necessary and the minutes of the Committee's meeting on 29 June 1971 report that 'the demolition contract had been awarded to L C Sams who would *pay the Association £35 for doing so.* Perhaps he knew a little more about the properties than the new owners.

Getting a suitable and viable development plan acceptable to the Local Authority was not quite so easy, not least because of our lack of experience. Fortunately, Ray Wilkins, the architect, had designed St Andrew's Court in Burnt Ash Lane and Norman Burke had been closely involved in several GLC housing schemes. The scheme eventually agreed, though attractive in its way and appropriate for the setting, was smaller than hoped for, providing only 16 self-contained bed-sitter flats, 2 larger one bedroom flats, communal lounge, guest room and warden's bungalow residence. At the time, self-contained bed-sitter flats, i.e. flats with separate kitchens and bathrooms but with a sleeping area as part of the main living room and a small store room, were considered adequate accommodation for older people living alone. Important features were that they were easily manageable, each had its own front door and there was a means of instant communication with the warden or her relief and somewhere else in the complex where residents could meet together. The one bed room flats were considered suitable for couples.

One benefit arising from the smaller than expected site coverage was the opportunity to create an attractive garden on to which every lounge would look out. That outlook also took in St Nicholas Church and its spire, a feature which Ray Wilkins doubtless had in mind in his careful design. Sadly he died before the building was completed and was unable to see how the residents appreciated it. The view from some of the kitchens, by contrast, was on to the Bull's Head garden which could be interesting on a hot summer evening!

A Development Subcommittee comprising four management committee members was set up to keep in close touch with the professionals throughout the design and development stage. This seems to have been the beginning of a subcommittee practice which has continued right up to the present time. Once the detailed plans and drawings were agreed and Bills of Quantities prepared by the Quantity Surveyors, the work was ready to go out to tender. A crucial factor was going to be as to whether the development as planned could be built within the Department of Environment yardstick allowance. If it could not, then changes would have to be made or the finance would not be forthcoming. Four firms were invited to tender for the contract and their tenders were opened excitedly at a meeting in Eric Bass' Marylebone office just a week before Christmas. One or two of these were wildly above the approved yardstick figure of £73,627 and the lowest from Wiffen of Plumstead was for £78,930. Before our hearts sank too far, we were advised by the Quantity Surveyor that the margin was not so great that it could not be eliminated by savings in the design. Norman Burke, who had obviously been in similar situations on GLC projects, was reassuring also and before long the two were recommending savings which brought the Wiffen tender figure down to £73,501. These savings were considered acceptable and, after a sigh of relief, we realised that the project could now go ahead and Wiffen would be the contractor.

It is obviously essential in all publicly financed projects for there to be adequate cost control and for there to be some kind of yardstick by which proposed expenditure can be measured. The yardstick was a fairly simple method of ensuring that housing associations and local authorities kept their costs to the minimum. It helped to ensure that the maximum number of housing units were provided out of the funds available. Nevertheless, savings made in order to keep within prescribed limits are not always in the long term interests of a project and can lead to higher running costs or other offsetting expenditure in later years. This was probably true to a small degree here and one or two of those savings were regretted later. Nevertheless, they allowed the work to go ahead and on 21 February 1972, the peace and quiet of Church Lane was disturbed as Wiffen diggers moved on to the site.

Now that the project was in the builders' hands, we did feel that we could give some publicity to the project and this was the time to let our friends and fellow Church members know what was going on. Although, thankfully, the main cost of the project was going to be met out of the Local Authority long term loan, we had realised that some fund raising was going to be necessary to cover costs outside the main development expenditure. This all pointed to a brochure linked to a stone laying ceremony.

It is amazing what a range of skills and talents can be found within one or two Church communities and what a blessing these can be when there is an interest in a project like this. One of the Park Road members at the time was the artist, Derek Waller - whose paintings and ceramics are now well known locally. He was interested in the project and voluntarily produced for us an attractively designed brochure which served not only to explain the project but also to publicise the stone laying ceremony fixed for Saturday 25 March 1972. This was to be followed by a 'short reception' in the Village Hall opposite for which admission was by ticket, 'price 10p'! (Intended to be two shillings - decimalisation had just arrived!)

The stone laying was a happy occasion. The builders were very co-operative and the 'foundation stone' was laid by Dr Barbara Morton, then 'Superintendent' of the Bermondsey Medical Mission - the organisation now known as Mission Care. Dr Morton, the 100th anniversary of whose birth is now being celebrated, was one of those remarkable Christian ladies whose achievements in care for the elderly and disabled had been an inspiration to a number of us. Her association with us at that moment was an encouragement and really marked the beginning of the friendly and co-operative relationship with the

Mission Care organisation which Cedarmore has enjoyed ever since. The ceremony was conducted by Rev John Doble, then minister of Crofton Baptist Church, who, on our behalf, committed the project to God for His blessing to be upon it. It was then time to leave the site to the builders and begin to plan how we should use the building which was going to be given to us.

That planning included agreeing terms of occupation, criteria for allocation of places, nature of warden supervision, form of garden landscaping, and furniture and equipment for communal facilities - most of which was allocated to small ad hoc subcommittees who enthusiastically made their recommendations. They were then given the task of putting most of those recommendations into practice. It was clear from the start that the garden was going to be important and the previous owner of the site generously provided a landscape plan for this which formed the basis of the garden layout which has always added to the attractiveness of the environment of this scheme. Margaret Duke and other ladies used their natural gifts to choose and acquire the furnishings for the communal lounge and guest room.

Perhaps the major task was to decide who were to be the first residents. Once building work had started and news of the project began to spread, enquiries as to eligibility for a place began to pour in. At one time it seemed that half the elderly people in Chislehurst living alone had applied! This gave us some difficulty as, in one sense, it was irrelevant to us that the project was in Chislehurst - it might equally have been in a less affluent part of the Borough. Moreover, during the months prior to starting the project we had acquired a list of elderly people mainly associated with our churches who really needed this kind of supportive accommodation. We also felt it to be incumbent upon us to give some priority to those of limited financial means - although it was soon evident that quite a few older people with reasonable financial resources needed this kind of provision almost as much. At that time the alternative of private sheltered or retirement housing was not available - it was several years before McCarthy and Stone and other house builders discovered this market! We were also conscious of our commitment to creating within the scheme, so far as possible, a 'caring Christian environment' and although this did not require all residents to be practising Christians it was important that prospective residents were aware of the ethos of the organisation. It seemed important also to spread the age and dependency range in view of the limited support which we should be able to provide. Somehow, the subcommittee concerned were able to take all these factors into account and decide on those who were to be offered the first places. In the event, the first residents were a combination of our own Church members, local residents and folk with special needs. Half the residents were over 80 and most of the others over 70. One much younger person to be offered a place was Morna Macfie, then 59, who also agreed to become the first relief warden. There were some misgivings over taking the oldest resident, the lovely 89 year old, Mrs Helen Green, but she settled in well and lived there happily without undue demands on the Warden until her death at the age of 93.

A more difficult exercise in one way was the recruitment of a Warden. These were the days before the person fulfilling that role became known as the 'Scheme Manager'. The role was also far more loosely defined that it is to-day. We were able to think of him or her as being like a very good neighbour to the residents as well as the one in charge of the property - and aware that an unhelpful appointment could have marred the whole scheme and not provided the atmosphere we were hoping to bring. The only member of our team who had had much experience in assessing suitability for a position such as this was Marion Wilmshurst, who had recently retired as Matron of the Dunoran Nursing Home,. Here, as on other occasions, she proved a blessing to us. After advertising nationally and locally and interviewing several people, the position was offered to Mrs Rita Fowler, a nurse with experience of caring for older people and a kind and caring nature. Although the scheme did not require the warden to be a nurse this seemed to be a bonus which helped to provide the caring atmosphere needed. In the event, although she stayed for only the first two years, Mrs Fowler turned out to have qualities which set the tone for the warden role which others following her were able to develop. Her husband Archie Fowler, himself almost 80 at the time also joined us and really enjoyed being part of the small community. He had been a professional cricketer and umpire and proved to be a popular character amongst both residents and local people.

An important decision which had to be made, of course, was the name for the scheme - a decision which sometimes can take hours to make! In this case, we had little difficulty in settling on 'Cedarmore Court' - which seemed appropriate enough - and the place has been known as such ever since.

The building contract provided for completion by Christmas that year and we, perhaps naively, thought we could assume that the building would be ready for occupation by the end of February. Plans were made for the Warden and several of the residents to move in during March and for an Official Opening on 3rd March 1973. In retrospect this was perhaps a little unfair on the builders and meant that, in the event, not all the flats were quite ready for occupation by that date and full practical completion was not certified until 23 March. Amazingly, relations with the builders remained good throughout and no one seemed to think it strange to have an official opening before completion! Perhaps it was put down to our naivety and over enthusiasm.

The Official Opening itself was a happy and memorable event attended by around 200 people in pleasant early March weather. After a short dedication service in the Village Hall opposite, led by Michael Walker, another local Baptist minister, the buildings were formally opened by John Hunt, the Bromley Member of Parliament at the time. John Hunt, as a good MP had encouraged us in this development and took a close interest in it. George Duke, then 80 and beaming more than ever, presided over the reception afterwards whilst Margaret served tea and refreshments for everybody. This time the charge was 20p! Although there was still much work to be done, we left in a celebratory mood, thankful and relieved that the planning and preparations of the previous months had at last reached fruition. Now we should be able to concentrate on the clients - the elderly people for whose benefit the whole project had been carried out.

Chapter 4
Cedarmore Court - A new Caring Community

It was a hectic time - those first few weeks as the builders put the finishes touches to all the building and residents gradually moved into the flats. A well attended housewarming party was held in the communal lounge in April and the group of twenty residents, sixteen ladies and four men, including two married couples, quickly came together as a small community. True, there were teething problems with the building - some found their flats too warm (this was the generation which had spent most of their lives without central heating!), the bathroom aids were inadequate the tarmacadam in the car park had not taken too well to the furniture vans and visitors to the neighbouring Bull's Head had very quickly found this an easy place for illicit parking! But within a few months, most came to see the development as a real success and few, if any, of the residents gave any impression of regretting having become part of this little community.

Why was this? Certainly, the planning had been thorough although much had been done in the spare time of the people concerned. Undoubtedly, it had benefited from the commitment and enthusiasm with which they embarked on this first project - and the support of the church communities behind them. It was a great help, too, to have a motherly caring person like Rita Fowler to guide and support the residents as they sought to adapt to their new environment. Another wise decision on the part of the management committee was to set up a small House Committee under Bryan Mendham to oversee the day to day running of the scheme. Specific responsibilities were then delegated to several individuals on that committee - the health and welfare of residents to Marion Wilmshurst, fabric problems to Don Mills and money matters to Roderick Caie. Celia Goyns became its secretary, producing its agendas and minutes, a task which she performed faithfully for the next 30 years! These five people regularly attended Bromley Baptist Church so that inevitably they occasionally found themselves discussing Cedarmore Court matters after a Sunday service! To make sure that nothing was overlooked, Margaret Duke, Janet Barret and one or two others formed a small group calling itself the Friends of Cedarmore Court which set out to ensure that living at Cedarmore Court could never become dull - remembering each resident's birthday, sometimes arranging tea parties and musical entertainment events. One of their first events was a summer garden party which not only introduced the residents to some of the supporters but also demonstrated the attractiveness of the new garden environment. Margaret and George Duke, ever lovers of hospitality, were in their element!

The spiritual welfare of residents was not overlooked either. Transport for Sunday morning Church services was generally available for those who wanted this and once a month on a Sunday afternoon a short service was held in the communal lounge - a practice which has continued right up to the present day.

Of course, it might be said that, with all this interest and support, the scheme was bound to be a great initial success but could that level of outside interest possibly be sustained? The answer, of course, is that it could not to that degree - as there were other demands on people's time and energies. Nevertheless, the structure for this support continued and has remained largely in place as different people have come along to take an interest in the scheme and the welfare of the residents. When Bryan Mendham moved from the area, Norman Burke himself took over leadership of the House Committee and the main responsibility for the running of this scheme, doing this for many years until it was handed over to Ron Dungate whose long and invaluable commitment to Cedarmore work is referred to later. When Marion had to give up her residents' welfare responsibility, this was taken on by Reiny Cooper and Audrey Richardson together and Audrey's husband, Ken, looked after the rents. Much support, too, has come from relatives of residents.

And what of the residents themselves? Looking back now at the thirty five years since Cedarmore Court opened, I believe it is fair to claim that, for almost the whole of that period, most residents have felt secure in that environment and content to spend some of their last years there. Some have been able to stay right to the end of their lives. For others, probably the majority, it became necessary to move on to residential or nursing care on reaching a stage of greater dependency. This reflects the limitations of the scheme, as discussed later, but not a failure to achieve its purpose. If statistics were to be compiled as to average age and length of stay, one might be surprised to discover how long some residents were able to live there. .Morna stayed for 25 years and Peggy for 18. Barbara, a much loved present resident, has now lived there for 25 years. Quite a few others have stayed for over 10 years.

Much could be said of the personalities of some of those early residents who were able to enjoy the Cedarmore Court amenities. Looking at the names of these, thoughts and memories of some interesting people come to mind. One of the first residents was Richard Furze, an 80 year old widower who had been a carpentry master and still liked to do a little woodwork as a hobby. He was allocated a ground floor flat near to a little space in the garden where it was possible to erect a small shed in which he could continue his hobby. The shed is still there to-day and used for storing garden tools, etc. Another of the early residents was Sidney Davis, who had been a solicitor's managing clerk. He loved to spend much of his day time in the Bromley Library, using the flat as his home base. There was Ivy Fluke from Pratts Bottom whose great problem over moving into Cedarmore was giving up her beloved cat. She wisely did so and found new companions (and birds to feed) there! There was Con Rogers, every inch a pre-war trained school teacher in her love of efficiency and propriety but with a heart of gold and a caring concern for her neighbour who was becoming 'confused'. One remembers Florence Treves, who subsequently moved into Beechmore, with her wicked sense of humour, and Barbara Jones whose passion for cleanliness occasionally disturbed her neighbour - and the two sisters, Phyllis and Joan, who were able to have flats next to each other - and others.

Much of the success of Cedarmore Court and the contentment

of its residents, though, has been due to the quality of the Warden (scheme manager) with which it has been favoured throughout its 35 years history. This is not always the experience of housing association schemes. Yet, even though the expectations from wardens and the job descriptions for this role have changed over the years, no one would deny how fundamental is their attitude and commitment to the success and whole atmosphere of a sheltered housing scheme. Although Rita Fowler stayed for less than two years, she set a pattern for the warden role at Cedarmore which has been continued and developed ever since. Over the subsequent 35 years up, there have been five other wardens, all blessed with supportive husbands interested in the work and the welfare of the community. Several of the husbands have helped with the gardens and general maintenance of the property. Reg Garthwaite, a retired master builder, not only kept an eye on this property but helped the Association in its other developments. One of the most loved of wardens was Mary Harding who held the position for over ten years. Mary had been on the Beechmore staff for a few years before taking over the Cedarmore Warden position on the retirement of Ivy Garthwaite. Mary had no aptitude for paper work which regrettably was finding a place in the Scheme Manager's duties but she loved to be with her residents and respond to their needs. She organised outings, theatre visits, even one or two holidays together - so much so that the social life of the residents became a talking point. On her retirement, the position was taken by Mina Coffey, whose husband, Bob, was a Baptist minister feeling the need for a change of occupation for a few years. Mina loved to serve people and Bob saw this and the other work he was able to do for Cedarmore as just another form of ministry. There was a sense of loss when they left after four years on Bob's accepting a call back to a pastorate.

Of no little value too, has been the presence on the site of a relief or assistant warden to take over during the warden's days off duty and holidays. Frequently, one of the residents has been employed in this role and, for much of the time; there has been someone with a nursing or caring background able to do this. Not only has this ensured that the warden has regularly had 48 hrs a week free from any responsibilities, it has enabled the scheme, with a little occasional outside help, to continue to provide on the site a 24 hour cover for emergencies (24/7 as it is now known). Many housing associations now rely upon community alarm schemes for this cover. Although this appears to work reasonably satisfactorily in most cases, it takes away the personal nature of the off duty support which many older people seem to value.

Readers of the above descriptions of the care and support which has gone into the work of Cedarmore Court may well conclude that the scheme and its residents have been particularly favoured. Many residents seem to have shared that view. Any local authority or company could have provided the accommodation and amenities, perhaps even better than Cedarmore did. What it probably would not have given are those special features which Cedarmore and its supporters were and have been able to provide, which I guess is illustrated above. It was a successful first scheme which gave great encouragement to its sponsors.

Yet, it did not take long after the opening for the limitations of Cedarmore Court in its ability to care for older people to become apparent. This presented a new challenge for the Association and how this was faced up to is the subject of later chapters.

Part II
THE SECOND PROJECT

Chapter 5
Another development

As the construction of Cedarmore Court was nearing completion towards the end of 1972 and as frantic preparations were being made at the beginning of 1973 for its opening and occupation, it began to dawn on members of the management committee that, as demanding as this project had been in a number of ways, it could not be the one and only development of Cedarmore Housing Association.

For one thing, they had been surprised by the interest shown in this one project by so many older people. Allocation of the eighteen places available had not been easy and it seemed likely that twice that number of places could have been filled without difficulty. No doubt this reflected the growing perception at the time that sheltered accommodation in some form was the answer to many older people's needs and distinctly preferable to residential care. But there were then only a few schemes of this kind in the area - a situation which was quite different ten years later.

Members had also learned a lot from this one project and discovered how the system worked. It would make sense to use some of that knowledge and experience in creating another scheme which would benefit more older people and be a practical service for our churches and for the local community.

The idea was aired at management committee within months from the opening of Cedarmore Court and there is a reference in the minutes to Bernard Cook proposing that nothing should be done about this until later in the year. Wise man as he was, he could see that time was needed to handle Cedarmore Court settling down matters and adequately assess that situation. In the event, the first serious discussion of the subject took place at the January 1974 meeting.

By that time, another relevant factor had emerged. A few of the residents who were accepted into Cedarmore Court at its opening had probably reached a degree of dependency which, in ordinary circumstances, would have ruled them out for a Category I sheltered housing scheme (as Cedarmore Court was later classified). They were not ready for residential care and had been keen to come to Cedarmore but before the end of the year it was clear that they really needed more help and supervision than was practicable in the unenclosed flats scheme there. This was before domiciliary care for older people became widely available and it imposed greater demands on the warden and relief warden than would probably be acceptable to-day.

The idea of another scheme which could cater for more dependant older people soon fastened in people's minds, therefore, and appeared to dominate the discussion at the January 1974 meeting, with some, including particularly Marion Wilmshurst, advocating a full residential care project . A small group was asked to investigate the possibility of this and did this expeditiously, reporting back two months later. Perhaps the early response was because they very quickly concluded that a full residential care project was not, at that time, a practical proposition, particularly from a financial point of view. No public finance for such a project was available. Private sector loan finance was not, then considered appropriate and no one had confidence that anything like sufficient funds could be raised charitably. The good news, though, was that grants were becoming available for Category II sheltered schemes (as they were then known) which could provide greater security and support for older people in an enclosed environment. Although this was far short of the residential care scheme which had been thought about (and which Cedarmore came back to several years later), it was unanimously accepted as the right way forward. The search for a second site was soon in progress.

In retrospect, one cannot but feel how wise that decision was and how in this Cedarmore was being led gradually towards the major residential project which it took on nearly ten years later. Much changed in those ten years, as the next chapter will reveal, and, with the limited experience and resources of both finance and people available at the time, it is probably unlikely that a Beechmore kind of project would then have got off the ground, or have been the remarkable success that Beechmore eventually turned out to be. In the event, the project which came out of this decision, Southmore Court, proved to be both a blessing in itself and an invaluable stepping stone along the way towards that greater responsibility.

But there was to be a waiting period before any such second development was to get off the ground - almost four years, in fact. Again, faith and patience were to be tested.

One of the first decisions was to choose an Architect. With the sad loss of Ray Wilkins, the Association really had little link with his London-based firm and the use of a smaller, more local firm was considered desirable. Bernard Cook suggested John Gill Associates of Eltham who had shown an interest in our objectives and so began the long involvement in Cedarmore schemes of Derek Bingham, then one of John Gill's senior staff. Derek had had experience in the planning of housing schemes and very quickly understood what we were looking for in a second sheltered scheme. He was familiar with Department of Environment standards which had to be complied with if public finance was to be available. He was also able to produce very quickly a sketch development plan for any site which became available.

Again potential development sites were not readily available and, as things turned out, there was really only one abortive feasibility study - a site in Sundridge Park which received serious consideration towards the end of 1974 but went elsewhere. At the beginning of 1975, however, at what appeared to be a chance encounter with one of the deacons of Southborough Lane Baptist Church, Cecil Lloyd learned that part of the land adjoining that small church might become available for development. Once more in the history of Cedarmore an unexpected encounter became the beginning of a major step forward.

Southborough Park Baptist Church, as it was then known, at that time comprised two small hut-like buildings erected in the 1930's on a quite large piece of land backing on to Petts Wood parkland. The Church congregation was expanding and urgently needed funds for the purchase of a manse for its minister and, later, for a new church building on the site. The site was large enough to incorporate both the new church building and a flats development. Cecil naturally thought that, if there was to be a flats development alongside the Church, why shouldn't that be the next Cedarmore development? Derek quickly produced a sketch plan showing how this could be done.

The Southborough Church congregation and leaders have strongly supported the Southmore Court project ever since it opened and have taken an active interest in the welfare of its residents. Indeed over the years, its minister and several of its members have been closely involved in the work of Southmore and frequent visitors to staff and residents. The Church and the sheltered scheme have become very close. In those early negotiations, though, the Church leaders didn't quite see it that way. Understandably they were a little wary of being drawn into a dual purpose arrangement when their sole objective in deciding to dispose of part of their valuable site was to maximise the funds available for the manse and building. The negotiations were interesting, therefore, and took some time to finalise. Indeed, they nearly floundered, mainly because Cedarmore was finding it difficult to find the site purchase moneys at the time they were required. Somehow, thankfully, the Church leaders and the vendors of the house being purchased for the manse remained patient and it became possible to secure the site long before details of the development could be agreed or building work started.

A 'Development Subcommittee' was again set up to agree the brief for the Architect and to pore over his plans. As well as pleasing us, Derek had to satisfy the Church, the Planning Authority and the newly formed Housing Corporation who were to provide the finance and to design a scheme which could be built within the stringent cost yardsticks which still prevailed.

Given this situation, what he eventually produced was undoubtedly a tribute to his design skills and to his detailed attention to the project. Its simple design and the compactness of the accommodation have made it an attractive building and a comfortable one for its residents. Making it a three-storey building (with a lift, of course) helped to maximise use of the site and provided some magnificent views over the parkland for the eventual residents. Even so, the approved plan was for only 20 self-contained flats, 19 bed sitter and 1 one bedroom, a warden's attached two bed roomed house, a communal lounge with small kitchen, a guest room and a laundry room. Bed sitter flats were then still considered the appropriate accommodation for single people in sheltered housing schemes. Its great advantage over Cedarmore Court from a security point of view was that all flats opened on to an internal corridor which gave direct access to communal amenities, including the warden's office, without going out of the building. The location of the communal lounge, close to the ground floor entrance and opening on to the garden, has been particularly beneficial and has helped to make this room the popular venue for residents that it has always been.

When Derek's plans were eventually agreed by all concerned, there was still the vital matter of finance to be settled. The Housing Corporation had in 1976 indicated that, in principle, they would be prepared to allocate funds for the scheme but they had financial problems of their own later that year and it was not until August 1977 that their funding was finally confirmed and the building project was able to go out to tender.

When the tenders were opened on 22 November, the lowest one was again from W F Wiffen, the company that had built Cedarmore Court. Again this was above the yardstick figure which had been agreed beforehand with the Housing Corporation and several design savings had to be made to bring their tender down to £242,085, a figure acceptable to the Corporation. Some of the savings would rather not have been made but they were essential if the scheme was to proceed. No time was then wasted. A building contract was signed on 22 February 1978 and Wiffens were on site by the end of the month. Unfortunately it was a very wet March and, with the heavy clay soil, much of the site soon became like a pond.

There was still plenty of water around when a stone laying ceremony was held on 22 April. This was preceded by a short service in the old Church building led by Donald Cranefield, by then minister of Bromley Baptist Church. In recognition of her strong commitment to this and the Chislehurst project and her many years of service for the elderly and disabled, Marion Wilmshurst had been invited to perform the stone laying and this she did admirably in spite of her own advancing years. The 'made up' private road alongside the site enabled the large group of supporters to watch the ceremony without going on the wet and muddy site! Don Mills then led the party into the Church Hall where, according to my copy of the programme, 'tea and biscuits were to be served by Joan Smith and her helpers'!

Much time was spent during the next twelve months in settling the details of the scheme and here the strength and expertise of some of the newer members of the Cedarmore team became apparent. Don Mills was able to discuss the heating and hot water arrangements with the heating subcontractors. Reg Shore looked into the call and fire alarm systems and the lighting proposals - just the beginning of so much that he was to give to Cedarmore over the next twenty five years. John Fagg agreed the décor and bent his ear to any building problem brought to his attention. Reg Knight, a recently retired District Tax Inspector and keen amateur gardener volunteered to design the garden and prescribe suitable plants. To-day nearly thirty years later, that design is still largely in place and enjoyed by residents. Derek Waller again designed the publicity brochure. How blessed Cedarmore was to have people of this caliber willing to give of their spare time to help make this project a success. Learning from the Cedarmore experience, a House Committee was also set up during this period and this helped greatly in planning administration matters in advance of completion, as well as in the selection of residents and appointment of the Warden.

The wet winter and spring was followed by a good summer and by the beginning of 1979 the building work was only seven weeks behind schedule. Most of that time was made up in the succeeding months so that the builders were able to hand the completed building over at the beginning of July, ready for its official opening on 21 July. In the meantime the Church had started and completed its new building on the site so that this could be used for the dedication service.

The Opening of Southmore Court, as this development was named, was a happy and memorable event for supporters, workers and incoming residents. By that time, Roger Sims had become Member of Parliament for Chislehurst, within which constituency the site just fell, and he readily accepted the invitation to perform the opening ceremony. Roger showed great interest in the project and so began his long interest in and support for the work of Cedarmore which has continued to this day. Donald Cranefield again led the service, joined by John Noddings, the recently appointed minister of the Southborough church.

The Church was full for the occasion, the congregation including many of the expected new residents and some of their relatives as well as supporters and others interested in the project. One memorable item on the programme was a rendering of the song 'Practical Praise' by Geoffrey Russell-Smith's youthful Revelation Choir. After the ceremonial opening at the entrance to the new building and the formal admission of two representative incoming residents, Eva Lawson and Herbert Harvey, there was much inquisitive roaming around the three stories followed by tea in the old church building, again in Margaret's capable hands.

But the mood of the day was perhaps best captivated in the opening hymn at the dedication service 'Now thank we all our God with hearts and hands and voices'.

So the second project was completed - in a way. Yet, as with all projects of this kind, opening of the new building was really only the beginning of a new work. Much had yet to be done to convert this new building into a place where older and frailer people would feel content and secure and part of the small Christian caring community which it became. How this was achieved and sustained right up to the present day is the subject of a later chapter. In the meantime, much had been happening in the sheltered housing world and in the legislative framework for its provision and it is worth pausing in the story to explain some of this to the reader.

Chapter 6
Keeping Pace with Change

The 1974 Housing Act was a somewhat unusual piece of legislation in that it was introduced as a Bill during Edward Heath's Conservative Government and passed into law as an Act of Parliament when Harold Wilson was leading the succeeding Labour Government, indicating its all party support. It was also a major step forward for the housing association movement, not least because it gave statutory recognition to housing associations, introducing a system of regulation and registration through a newly created body, the Housing Corporation. The Corporation was also to be the body through which Central Government could channel funds for housing association developments instead of through Local Authorities.

The first Chairman of the Housing Corporation was Lord Goodman, a friend of both Edward Heath and Harold Wilson, known more perhaps for his skills in negotiation and arbitration rather than in administration. He was greatly gifted in persuasion and, once he saw the benefits which could come from the extension of affordable housing through housing associations, he used those skills to persuade the Government to make large sums of money available to the Corporation for use in that way. The result was a proliferation of housing association schemes of all kinds, including many designed for the elderly. The years 1975 - 1985 were probably the heyday for the housing association movement. After that, there was much greater emphasis on achieving value for money and using private sector finance. So many commitments appear to have been made in those first few years that the Corporation had to call a 'moratorium' on its funding of new schemes for a while in 1977. The Southmore Court project was caught in that moratorium causing a short delay and some anxiety in the pre-tender period.

Funding from the Housing Corporation took the form of both Loan and Grant, the grant, in most cases, forming by far the larger part. It was a method quite favorable to housing associations. At the beginning of a scheme, once it was approved, all funds required came by way of temporary loan - to cover site acquisition, building costs and professional fees - thus enabling the work to proceed as soon as a tender could be accepted within the approved yardstick figure. Once the scheme was completed and the total allowable costs, rental income and expected running costs of the development could be ascertained, the net rental income was capitalised at the prevalent interest rate, geared to Bank Rate, and that capitalised sum became the amount of the 60 year loan to the Association. The remainder of the temporary loan was converted into a Housing Association Grant (HAG) only repayable if the property were sold or failed to serve a social housing project. At the time of the Southmore Court completion in 1979, interest rates were very high and the relevant rate was 15%. The effect was that, of the total allowable expenditure on the scheme of £340,000, £295,000 was provided by Grant and only £45,000 by long term loan. Several casual readers of Cedarmore published Accounts in later years have expressed surprise that money should have been borrowed at as high a rate of 15% - not appreciating that, had the rate used have been lower, the loan principal would have been greater, the grant smaller and the interest payable just the same! Such was the generous funding system at that time. There was still around £5,000 which Cedarmore had to find itself through donations and small fund-raising to cover inadmissible and amenities expenditure - not an undue burden by comparison with subsequent fund raising needs.

This was also the time when the system of fair rents and housing benefits came into operation. Local Rent Officers agreed maximum fair rents for each flat in a development, reviewing these every two or three years, sometimes setting them higher than those asked for by the housing association. There was little incentive for keeping them lower; however, as provided they did not exceed the Rent Officer's figures, full Housing Benefit was available to assist low income residents. Not surprisingly, this system increased the paperwork and was another step in the march towards the bureaucratizing of housing association activities - but it did ensure that very limited means was no barrier to admission to a housing association scheme.

The 1974 Act also introduced a system of Revenue Deficit Grant whereby an income shortfall, as measured by specified standards, could be recovered from Central Government. This was a great help to struggling housing associations, enabling them to keep solvent at a time when inflation was rampant, but it was hardly a great incentive to efficiency. In practice, as the fair rents regime developed and higher rents were registered, some associations were able to accumulate surpluses. It was not surprising, therefore, that from 1980 onwards; they were required to transfer such surpluses to a Grant Redemption Fund which gave the Housing Corporation some control over their use. Cedarmore was never in that position!

This was the financial and developing bureaucratic climate in which the Southmore Court development reached its fruition. One of its effects, of course, was to increase the time which Committee members were obliged to give to administrative and financial matters when perhaps they would rather have been more directly involved with the people they were serving. It was still many years before the Association had any administrative staff, other than the scheme wardens. Fortunately, it was blessed with several new management committee members and the newly formed Southmore Court House Committee brought some very committed and energetic people into the team. It is perhaps time to relate some of the internal changes which had taken place.

The first chairman of the Association, George Duke, who had greatly encouraged the team in its early days and in the development of Cedarmore Court, died in 1974 at the age of 81. The Management Committee minute recording his death refers to 'his dedicated and enthusiastic leadership over the past five years and wise counsel ' and 'gives thanks to God for the example of Christian service and integrity so manifest in his life'. His widow Margaret continued to support, and encourage the work in various ways. John Barrett, then probably the youngest member of the Committee, was appointed Chairman in his place but was obliged to relinquish this position a year or so later owing to overseas business commitments. These caused him to leave the committee altogether a few years later but it is interesting to record than , soon after he retired from business altogether in 2002, John accepted an invitation to rejoin the Management Committee and shortly afterwards took over the major role of chairman of the Residential Care Executive. Cecil Lloyd succeeded John as Chairman and held this position for nearly ten years, bringing to it his keen intellect and his many years of experience in the legal profession and in voluntary work. He was succeeded by Norman Burke in 1985, to whom we have already referred.

Other early members of the Committee had been obliged to retire for various reasons. Harold Redknap, Gilbert Jones and Norman Foy had died. Alan Silcox, Jim Drummond, Dewi Jenkins, Graham Ratcliff and, later, Bernard Cook, had moved out of the area. It is perhaps remarkable how readily other talented people came along to join the Cedarmore team and give valuable service for many years afterwards. Was it perhaps because they were of the generation who willingly gave voluntary service for a cause which they thought worth while or because of their Christian commitment - or, more likely, both? Apart from Reg Shore, John Fagg, Don Mills and Reg Knight, to whom earlier reference has been made, those joining in the work around this time included, Brian Cooper, Douglas Thomas and Norma Castle. Brian, whose mother had spent her last few years at Cedarmore Court, chaired the Southmore House Committee for twenty years and gave invaluable service to so many of its residents. Douglas became its Secretary almost from the start and has continued to give that service right up to the present day. Amongst many other things, his copper plate writing skills have helped on numerous occasions! Norma began regularly visiting residents at Southmore in 1979 and occasionally relieving the Warden to allow her to leave the premises for short periods. She has continued to do this ever since and not many weeks go by when she is not seen in the lounge one afternoon chatting to residents.

So, notwithstanding the changes, the work of Cedarmore was able to continue and expand and adapt to the new regulatory climate. A further intake of helpers came as the Beechmore scheme was being planned in 1983 onwards. We are not yet ready to discuss that project but it is time to observe just how the Southmore Court scheme developed after its enthusiastic opening in July 1979.

Chapter 7
Southmore Court - A Thriving Community

Two major tasks during the construction period, apart from making sure that the building and its amenities were going to meet the requirements, were the allocation of places to potential residents and the appointment of Warden and Relief Warden. These were time absorbing responsibilities but very fulfilling for those involved. As previously, ad hoc subcommittees were set up for these tasks.

With the Cedarmore Court experience in mind, the importance of the Warden appointment to the success of the scheme was recognised from the start. The two bedroom house joined to the building could accommodate two people without difficulty. It linked up to the flats through an intermediate Warden's office and this avoided any need for her to go out of the building to visit a resident or vice versa.

It was also recognised that a relief warden resident on the premises was going to be needed both to ensure that full 24 hour cover was provided and that the Warden had adequate time off duty, away from the premises if she wished. To make such cover practicable even with a resident relief warden was sometimes not easy but, in those early years at least, it was nearly always possible to fill any gaps through voluntary help. This showed the value of the Church and local support for the project. It would make quite a difference to the Warden's life if there were folk she could call upon to hold the fort for a short while when she needed to pop up to the shops or make an urgent visit.

We did not have to look far for the first relief warden. Amongst the potential residents, and one very much in need of housing accommodation, was Kathleen, a lady who had for several years been in charge of a local Bermondsey and Brook Lane Medical Mission residential care home. Her experience made her an ideal candidate for the relief warden position and she was able to exercise that role for several years.

Appointing the Warden herself took a little longer - but this likewise seemed to come without great difficulty. Advertisements for the post were placed early in 1979 and amongst those responding was Lorna Rutty, a lady with a warm and caring nature, who had had both administrative and caring experience. Although probably capable of a greater responsibility, she felt a strong attraction to this position, and it did not take the subcommittee long to conclude that this was another gift to us and that Lorna would provide just what the project needed to convert it into the caring community hoped for. Their only concern was as to how long she would stay in the position before feeling a call to greater responsibilities. In the event she stayed for three years, leaving only to get married and move to Southampton. During that time she proved a tremendous blessing and helped to set up the scheme both to run efficiently and give residents the welcome and sense of security which they needed. It was an indication of the affection with which she had come to be regarded that quite a few of the residents as well as several committee members went down to Southampton to her wedding to Edwin Bird in September 1982.

News of the nature of the Southmore Court scheme had spread rapidly in the locality and in local churches whilst the building was under construction. At the January 1979 Management Committee meeting it was reported that 77 enquiries had been received, of which 45 were serious applications for places. One of the conditions of the Grant for the project was that the Local Authority was to have the right to nominate 50% of the residents from their own waiting list - a condition to which one could hardly object. Fortunately, at least five of the applicants were also on the Council's waiting list and the Council was quite happy to nominate these as part of their share. Even so this still meant that places could be offered to no more than 10 out of the remaining 40 serious applicants and fresh applications continued to arrive. Criteria for selection had been set by management committee but deciding on those ten people was no easy task for the subcommittee. Most applicants, including those nominated by the Local Authority were visited by two Cedarmore representatives before the decisions were made. In the event, the elderly people who began to move into the building after 19 July turned out to be an interesting group of older citizens, diverse in their backgrounds and characters, with different tastes and interests. All seemed grateful to be there and surprisingly, thanks no little to Lorna's shepherding, soon began to be a small sharing community.

As at Cedarmore, men were in the minority - only four out of the 21 residents. Less than half had a close Church association but this did not seem to create a division and all seemed to appreciate the unobtrusive caring Christian environment which Lorna and Kathleen and the House Committee were attempting to create. Personalities who spring to mind when thinking of those first residents are May Parsons, with her tough exterior and heart of gold, Eva Lawson who loved to feed the birds and the fine George Milnes who attended Mass most days at the nearby Catholic Church and was sadly knocked over by a passing vehicle when crossing the road. Several of those early residents stayed at Southmore until they died. At least six subsequently moved on to Beechmore after it opened in 1986 and ended their lives there

One practice at Southmore Court from the start was the provision of a midday cooked meal twice a week for residents, in the communal lounge. This was optional but soon became popular and one of those occasions, like the coffee mornings, when residents came together and got to know each other. For many years this was provided by voluntary helpers who would cook much of the meal at home before bringing it to Southmore. Later Health and Safety regulations brought an end to that practice! For several years now, it has not been possible to find volunteers to provide this service but the practice has continued, with the Scheme Manager and her assistant themselves cooking the meals, with some help from one or two residents. This twice weekly eating together remains an enjoyable feature of Southmore to this day. The practice was helped, of course, by the enlargement of the kitchen which was carried out in 1994.

Another practice which started under Lorna and has been continued by her worthy successors is the regular celebration of birthdays and special events by teas or small parties in the lounge or garden and this has all contributed to the friendly community atmosphere which has made Southmore such a popular place.

Much could be said of Southmore Court as a model Category II sheltered housing scheme and certainly it has been described in that way on numerous occasions. Looking back now on its nearly 30 years history, it is really difficult not to see it like that and as a very successful project. The best criterion, of course, is as to the contentment of its residents - and the approval of their families. From all accounts, by that judgment it has scored full marks for most of the time - not least in recent years when many have wanted to go there, notwithstanding most of the accommodation still being in bed sitter flats. What accounts for this?

Foremost, perhaps, is the quality of staff, Southmore has been able to retain throughout that period. Lorna was succeeded by Doris and Doris by Nora. Although both stayed for only a few years, they built on the foundation laid by Lorna and continued the practices which she had initiated. Both brought nice husbands into the picture and this provided several bonuses - and the occasional conflict of interest! On Nora's retirement in 1988, Kay joined the staff and brought to the position her organising and administrative skills as well as a watchful concern for the welfare of all residents. She stayed for 17 years, participating in the general professionalising of sheltered scheme staff, joining as the Warden and leaving as the Scheme Manager! She participated eagerly in several building and amenity improvements, including the extension, which took place during that period and, whilst demanding high standards from tradesman and outside bodies with whom she had contact, she gave assurance and security to residents. Kay was succeeded by Ros who has continued in the same vein, caring for each resident and looking for opportunities to bring interest and colour into the their lives - even to leading summer holiday parties to seaside resorts!

Important, too, has been the good relations which the Warden has had, at most times, with families of residents and the enlisting of their co-operation in dealing with small problems which occasionally arise. Most have recognised the benefit that Southmore has brought to their parent or relative and have often demonstrated this by participating in some of its events.

No less, perhaps, has been the regular involvement of voluntary supporters, including those on the House Committee and others who have supported special events and visited residents. It seems to have added to the sense of security and well-being of most residents to know that there are a group of people behind a project who voluntarily take an interest in their welfare and are responsible for the success of the scheme. They actually meet these people from time to time so that there is no faceless bureaucracy making decisions on their welfare. Foremost, in relation to Southmore Court, perhaps has been the quiet thoughtful role of Brian Cooper, both as Chairman of the House Committee for many years and as the person who visited at least once a week to collect rents, as necessary, help with Housing Benefit claims, etc and generally chat with residents. Not surprising perhaps that they gave him a generous present and farewell tea party when his own health caused him to give up this service after doing it for 28 years!

Helpful, too, has been the close relationship which has developed over the years with the neighbouring Church and its minister and the regular interest which they have shown in the welfare of the residents. Once a month on a Sunday afternoon, a service is held in the Southmore Court lounge - a practice which started in 1979 and has continued ever since. Not all residents attend this, of course, but it does emphasise the Christian foundation on which the project is based and brings a reminder that there can be spiritual as well as material blessings in old age.

Southmore Court is one of the minority of sheltered housing schemes which still provide what is now called 24/7 warden cover on site for its residents. Most now rely upon community alarm schemes for evening, night and weekend cover and these can be reasonably satisfactory. Nevertheless, most older residents, it seems, still prefer the personal cover which Southmore provides. This comes at a cost, of course, - a situation which can bring its problems to-day.

But did this undoubtedly successful Southmore Court scheme achieve the objectives which the Cedarmore committee had in mind when deciding upon a second development back in 1974? The answer to this comes in the next chapter.

PART III
EXTRA CARE

Chapter 8
A New Vision

It is perhaps surprising that, within a year from the successful completion of the Southmore Court scheme, the Cedarmore team were beginning to think of a third project with full residential care in mind. The suggestion is referred to in minutes of a management committee meeting in June 1980 as a third development in the form of 'a small Part III home' and it was agreed to consider the need for this at a later meeting. At the October meeting there was a paper on the subject for discussion and the minute reads 'it was generally agreed that this was a desirable objective if it were within the resources and capabilities of the Association to achieve this'. It also went a little further and decided to discuss the possibility at a special meeting in the following March to which house committee members and others would be invited. The invitation seemed to be widened further and in the event was attended by around 50 people. That meeting at Southmore Court on 10 March 1981 strongly supported the idea and this proved to be a vital first step in the development of an 'extra care project', as it became known.

Six years previously, the management committee had ruled out the possibility of developing and managing any kind of residential care project. What had happened since then to bring about this change of attitude? There seem to have been several factors leading to this. Undoubtedly the success of the Southmore project and the high demand for places there had increased confidence in their ability to carry through new developments. As we have noted, several new people had joined both management and house committees and this had infused new enthusiasm into the work. But the main factor was the early realisation that there would always be some people who would need a degree of care which it was not possible to provide in a sheltered housing situation. Notwithstanding the high quality of warden care which was now being provided at both Cedarmore Court and Southmore Court through Ida Drew and Lorna Rutty and their assistants, it was clear that some of the residents there would sooner or later need to move on to some form of residential or nursing care. Marion Wilmshurst with her years of nursing experience had foreseen this, of course, and was amongst the keenest advocates of the new vision.

Cedarmore were not alone in beginning to think along these lines. Others were coming to similar conclusions. The Abbeyfield movement which for years had promoted small Abbeyfield houses with just one warden or manager in charge had started to promote 'extra care' schemes for their frailer residents. Housing associations involved in sheltered housing for the elderly were discussing the problem although only a few went so far as to develop residential schemes, there being some reluctance to take on the closer management responsibility involved. Several churches or church groups were responding to needs of their elderly people in this way. Committee members had heard of successful schemes at Ealing and Romford and of new developments proceeding at West Ham and Frinton through local churches. All this gave encouragement to Cedarmore people to go further down this road.

The response of management committee to the enthusiastic endorsement of the idea at the March 1981 meeting was to set up a 'Steering Committee' to take the idea further. Its brief to that committee was wide and positive –

To proceed with the general planning of a project to provide extra care for around 15 to 20 elderly people with Cedarmore and Southmore residents and Church members or associates particularly in mind but without authority to enter into any commitment.

To explore sites or properties which might become available
To explore and plan ways of raising the necessary finance for such project
To promote interest and support for such project amongst members and leaders of participating churches and to seek to measure the support therefore

Not surprisingly, nearly half the management committee went on to that committee initially and were joined by both wardens and one or two new Church representatives. Its existence, however, did enable the project to be considered, planned and promoted outside normal management committee business and without distracting attention from ongoing management of the two sheltered schemes.

The new committee set about its work very quickly and within a few months they had adopted general guidelines as to the nature and size of the project, explored the property market and considered one or two potential sites, canvassed possible support for such a project from a number of local churches and considered ways of raising the finance.

Apart from the work of the two scheme wardens, the Association was still being run by a small group of people in their spare time. In retrospect, their confidence in deciding to take this further step and develop a project bound to involve so much more commitment and responsibility than the two sheltered schemes was quite remarkable. However, by now there was a firm conviction that this was the right way forward for them and that, if this was so, the resources needed in site, personnel and finance would become available in due time. As the next chapters will show that conviction turned out to be right and, over the next few years, step by step those needs were met and a project was completed which has proved a blessing to many people ever since.

Chapter 9
Locating the Site

The location for a project of this kind was very relevant. It needed to be within the London Borough of Bromley, of course, and preferably within easy distance from the two sheltered schemes and not too far from the supporting churches. However, then as now, good building sites were not readily available. Attractive ones were likely to be taken by private developers or by other housing associations who were now active in promoting new general and sheltered housing schemes in the area. It seemed there would need to be some special circumstances if Cedarmore were to find a site suitable for their new project.

For a short while there was serious interest in a property in Mavelstone Road which had considerable land and was ready for redevelopment. The Architect produced sketch plans for this which were even submitted for outline planning consent. Fortunately in retrospect, that consent was refused. Its location was by no means ideal and it did not compare in suitability with the site which eventually became available. How the Southlands Road site became available to Cedarmore is a story in itself.

It was August Bank Holiday Saturday morning when the secretary was returning from a brief visit to Southmore Court and his drive back took him down Oldfield Road and Southlands Road, past the old Homefield Nursing Home building at the junction with Southborough Road. He knew the building and observed the long garden fence going well down Southlands Road. The site situation had doubtless been on his mind and the thought occurred to him - does Homefield with its very frail residents really need a garden of this length? Would they not in fact be pleased to be relieved of the responsibility for maintaining it? If so, would they be interested in selling it to Cedarmore? Homefield was owned by Bermondsey and Brook Lane Medical Mission (now Mission Care) with whom Cedarmore had always had friendly relations and the Secretary knew Ken Wallace, its then General Secretary, well. That afternoon he telephoned Ken at his home, found him remarkably encouraging and was invited to come round and discuss the matter at his home on the Bank Holiday Monday afternoon. So began a quite long period of discussion and negotiation which led to this site becoming the location for the new project - a site suitable and convenient in a number of ways and truly a gift to Cedarmore.

The Homefield property was actually owned by the Special Trustees of Guys Hospital, the Mission having only a lease of it. Ken Wallace clearly had a good relation with them and offered to raise the matter with them straightaway. Their immediate response, though cautious, was also encouraging, sufficiently so for the steering committee to invite the Architects to produce a sketch plan showing how this site could be developed to provide a scheme of the kind and size envisaged. These were discussed and generally approved and shown to the Trustees for their consideration.

Early in 1982, they indicated that they would be prepared to sell the site to Cedarmore for the purpose of this development if planning consent could be obtained, the price to be based on their surveyor's valuation. Cedarmore commissioned David Connolly, an experienced local surveyor and friend, to value the site for them, based on the proposed development, and his figure was £67,500. On 2nd June Cedarmore received a letter from the Special Trustees' Surveyors formally offering, on their behalf, to sell the site to Cedarmore, subject to planning consent, for £70,000 - their valuation figure.

The Management Committee met on 11 June at 8 pm and this site offer was, of course, the most important item on the Agenda. It was a memorable meeting and for several on that committee a stressful one. It was one of those few occasions in the history of the Association when the Committee was seriously divided - in this case between 'the businessmen' and 'the enthusiasts'. The former felt strongly that Cedarmore should not pay more for the site than their own surveyor's valuation. The enthusiasts felt that it was ridiculous to risk losing this site and the unique opportunity which it offered for the sake of £2,500 - a small figure in relation to the eventual total costs of the development. For once an actual vote had to be taken and the business men won by one vote. And, as it turned out, they were proved to be right! But the Secretary did not sleep well that night.

The Committee's decision was duly conveyed to Ken Wallace and to the Trustees and, after an anxious week or so, to the delight of the Committee and surprise of some, a letter was received back confirming that the Trustees would accept £67,500 for the site, if outline planning consent was sought immediately. What led the Trustees to accept the Cedarmore figure has never been disclosed. Their sympathy and that of the Mission with the objectives of the scheme was undoubtedly a factor.

Whether the brinkmanship in the Cedarmore response was really justified in the circumstances could be debated still. It certainly avoided valuation problems later.

However, the situation now was that, provided planning consent could be obtained, we now had a very attractive site ready for the new project. Our doubts and divided opinions had been overruled.

A planning application was now the priority. By this time, Derek Bingham had branched out into practice on his own and we were happy that he should take over this project. He immediately set about turning the sketch plans into an outline planning application which was submitted in September. There was some local comment and a few amendments had to be agreed but the Association received a splendid Christmas present when the project received Outline Planning Consent on 23 December 1982.

So the New Year offered great prospect of the project proceeding. There was just the small problem of financing it and this is the subject of the next chapter.

Before proceeding to that subject, however, it is perhaps worth pondering on the key role which Ken Wallace, perhaps, unknowingly, played in this development. Without his approachability, encouragement, introduction to the owners and possible intervention the site might never have been acquired. Ken was a member of Bromley Baptist Church and had joined the Bermondsey Mission staff on retirement from the Bank of England. By the time the project was completed in March 1986, he had retired from the Mission also and offered to help voluntarily two or three days a week in the reception office at Beechmore, which he did for several years. He had been an officer in Montgomery's Eighth Army during the Second World War and had retained a degree of military style and discipline. Notwithstanding this he became much liked by staff and residents and a real help to the Home. After his health failed a few years later, he actually became a resident of the Home, living there for several years until his death in 1999. It is nice to feel that the project which he had helped to bring about became a comfort to him at his time of need.

Chapter 10
Finding the Money

When in March 1981 the management committee decided in principle to plan a small extra care development, they were still under the impression that there was little prospect of public finance for this being available. They assumed that most likely it would have to be financed through charitable funding and loans. Even a year or so later when they were contracting to purchase the Southlands Road site, it was assumed that the site cost would have to be met through charitable funding. It was welcome news, therefore, when in early 1982 the possibility of Housing Corporation finance for some kind of residential schemes began to emerge.

Housing Corporation funds came through the Department of Environment who set the criteria for their use and the standards of the schemes which they would support. Their emphasis naturally was on 'housing' and there was a reluctance to sponsor projects which required considerable support or care costs subsequently. Nursing home projects, for example, have never been able to receive capital funding from this source. In around 1981, when the need for more housing schemes with some degree of support for people with special needs was becoming apparent, the Housing Corporation began to open its door to applications for funding such projects.

These were deemed to include 'caring hostels for the elderly' and one or two housing associations were able to take advantage of this assumption to obtain funding towards schemes which provided residential care, one of the first of which was Burrows House in Penge.

Cedarmore's first approach to the Corporation in the form of an enquiry received a not discouraging response. A formal Bid to be included in a funding allocation was submitted but this could not be considered until there was a scheme which had outline planning consent. A further approach was made soon after Christmas 1982 when the Outline Planning Consent had been received. This was followed very shortly by a telephone call to say that the Area Manager would like to see the site for himself. This friendly and unassuming man visited Homefield a week or so later, saw only Ken Wallace and the Secretary and discussed the site and the proposed development with them, showing interest in its objectives. He seemed to like the proposal and suggested that a formal application for Outline Approval of funding be submitted as soon as possible. Such application required some detailed information, including costings from the Quantity Surveyors, but somehow it was submitted by 20 January. After one or two meetings with Corporation staff at Croydon, an Advance of funds for the project was formally approved on 31 March 1983.

Understandably, there was rejoicing in Cedarmore quarters that Easter. How was it that they were so blessed? Their prayers were again being answered - the channel this time being a civil servant who had made a timely visit. It was later learned that the funds set aside for this project were 'slippage monies' which had not been drawn upon as expected and needed to be allocated to a scheme in that financial year to avoid their being lost. If that visit had not been made and the slippage monies not been available, it could have been several years before other funding was available. It so happened, that Cedarmore had received a monitoring visit from Corporation officers in the previous November. Perhaps their report helped too. But, looking at Beechmore Court years later, it is humbling to remember that this project was built largely on 'slippage monies'!

As part of the understanding with the Housing Corporation, Cedarmore committed itself to providing £100,000 towards the cost of the scheme from charitable funding.

A fundraising group was set up, therefore, under the leadership of Elizabeth and Andrew Ghinn and, with the help of an attractive brochure again designed by Derrick Waller, they began to appeal to various Trusts, Churches and individuals for contributions towards this and organise a few fundraising events. From one source and another over a period of time they successfully raised this sum.

In the event, the Housing Corporation funds, by way of loan and grant, covered most of the basic costs of the building - site purchase, professional fees and building contract. Considerable expenditure on equipment, furniture, etc was necessary so that the building could serve its purpose and the charitable funds were used for this and for helping with staff accommodation.

So, in April 1983, Cedarmore found itself in the favoured position of having an attractive site, with outline planning consent for its scheme, a commitment to fund its basic costs subject to detailed approval, and a team of enthusiastic people committed to working to bring the project to fruition. There was much yet to be done as the next chapters will show but in the Cedarmore camp there was a great sense of 'Ebenezer' and feeling that, with that same help, something really worthwhile was going to be achieved.

Chapter 11
Building the House

By Easter 1983 the management committee realised that a crucial stage in this project had been reached and it was time to review the situation. A joint meeting with the Development Committee (as the Steering Committee had now been named) was held on 18 April and together they contemplated the major task now before them. It could have been seen as formidable but this was not the mood. Rather they carefully considered the various aspects of the work and noted who was taking responsibility for these.

The initial major task was to complete and agree the detailed design of the building. Until this was settled, little work on planning how to use it to provide residential care could proceed. The major responsibility for this, of course, fell on the Architect and Derek set about this task with enthusiasm and commitment. He also needed a measure of patience and understanding. So far little more than the size and configuration of the proposed building had been agreed and he was required to use his professional skills to work out how this could be used to serve the intended purpose.

In so doing he had many people to please. As well as satisfying his client (who occasionally spoke with more than one voice!), the plans and specification had to be acceptable to the Housing Corporation and to Social Services as well as the Planning Authority. Fortunately he was the kind of architect who welcomed hearing his client's comments and appreciated the input which John Fagg, Reg Shore and others were able to give. He was also familiar with Dept of the Environment building standards with which the project had to comply.

Arising from a general recognition in the country that standards of accommodation for people in residential care had to improve, a Registered Homes Bill was then going through Parliament which became the Registered Homes Act 1984. This would require all homes for elderly people with more than five residents to be registered with the Local Authority and to meet minimum space and other standards. Although those standards were no higher than Cedarmore would have wanted to apply in any case, it was another factor which had to be borne in mind at this planning stage.

Finally, of course, he had to watch the cost, knowing that this had to be kept within a Dept of Environment 'total indicative cost' figure, or very close to it, if the Corporation were to provide funding. This necessitated keeping in close touch with the Quantity Surveyors.

Notwithstanding all these factors, by the end of June Derek had drawings ready and agreed with the Development Committee and was able to apply for Detailed Planning Consent from the Local Authority. Shortly afterwards, the details were ready to go to the Housing Corporation with the Quantity Surveyor's cost estimates. There were a few months of waiting whilst various points were debated but by the end of the year the scheme had received detailed planning consent and, early in January 1984, the Housing Corporation 'design stage' approval also. Could they soon start building? Well, not quite yet - as anyone involved in a building project would know.

Much work had still to be done on working drawings, bills of quantities, arrangements for the major services to the building and other matters. After all this had been completed, the building project was ready to go out to tender and the Committee met on 3 July to consider a list of recommended contractors. This was no small contract and Cedarmore had to be sure that those tendering had the resources to carry the work through. Six firms were invited to tender and were given six weeks in which to do so. Careful arrangements were made for a tender opening at the Quantity Surveyors office in Baker Street on Thursday afternoon 30 August. Those closely involved in the project to date could now go for their summer holiday!

There is always something exciting about a Tender Opening and the carefully laid down procedures for this add drama to it. This one was no exception, not least because of the importance of one of the tenders coming close to the TIC figures.

In the event, all six figures were reasonably close, there being less than 1% difference between the two lowest tenders. This meant waiting for the Quantity Surveyors' closer examination of these two tenders before one could be sure as to which one was acceptable. However, both of these looked as if they would give an acceptable total costs figure and this made the journey back from the West End a cheerful one. A week later a satisfactory Report was received from the Quantity Surveyors and, on their recommendation, when the management committee met on 14 September they agreed to accept the tender of £438,031 from Whyatt Builders Limited for this work. A building contract with them was signed shortly afterwards.

Sadly, at this same meeting of the management committee the resignation from the committee of Marion Wilmshurst, on account of her failing health, had to be accepted. Marion had been an inspiration behind the extra care project from the start and an advocate of high standards. Perhaps this was a fitting moment for her to leave, knowing there was little now that could prevent the project going ahead. Little did she realise then that, by the time the building was completed and the home ready for occupation, her health would have deteriorated to the extent that she herself needed residential care. In fact she became one of its earliest residents and lived there happily until her death a few years later.

By now the building needed a name and, not surprisingly, this took a little time to resolve! However, one prominent feature of the Homefield garden of which this site had been part was a lovely old beech tree. Sadly it stood quite in the way of the proposed new building and the Local Authority gave permission for it to be removed provided that a new beech tree was planted in its place when the building had been completed. In the light of the names given to the two previous Cedarmore developments, it seemed logical to call this one 'Beechmore Court' and so it has been known ever since - perhaps often shortened to just 'Beechmore'.

Whyatts moved on to the site on Monday 5 November - a significant date perhaps but not an ideal one for starting a new building. But the weather was reasonable and they were able to make sufficient progress with foundation work for a stone laying ceremony to be held on Saturday afternoon 24 November. This proved to be a memorable occasion as folk who had supported the project or kept in touch with developments were now able to see it becoming a reality. There was now no going back. Roger Sims MP, who by now had become a good friend of Cedarmore and interested in its work laid the foundation stone with the inscription *'Hic Dabo Pacem'* (in this place I will give peace) - expressing the sincere wishes of all those who had been involved in the project to date. The ceremony on site was followed by a short service in Bromley Baptist Church led by Donald Cranefield attended by more than 50 people and ending with the hymn 'Lord of all Hopefulness'. Perhaps the apt words of that hymn echoed the prayers and aspirations of those present.

The project was now in the hands of the builders and the architect - and, perhaps one other person, Reg Garthwaite. Reg was the husband of Ivy who had recently taken over as Warden at Cedarmore Court on the retirement and return to Yorkshire of Ida and Stanley Drew. He had been a master builder and was close to retirement age. He had already been of assistance at Cedarmore on one or two building problems and it was obvious that there was little that he didn't know about the building trade. Although not absolutely essential, it was thought that it would be helpful to have a Clerk of Works on the site during the building contract who would see everything that was going on and work closely with the Architect. Reg seemed an ideal person for this role. He was interested in the project and readily accepted our suggestion, giving to it far more than we expected, for very modest remuneration. This worked out remarkably well. He soon developed a good relationship with both the Whyatt staff and the Architect and they had confidence in him. At the end of the contract, he probably knew more about the building than anyone else and this proved a great help to us in the early days of its occupation. Reg was another of those unexpected blessings which came to Cedarmore during the development of the Beechmore project.

The building contract was expected to last just over twelve months and during this period there was a great deal for the Development Committee and others to attend to if the building was to serve its intended purposes. How they were able to do this is the subject of the next few chapters.

Chapter 12
Preparing for Beechmore

As members of the development committee returned home from the Stone Laying service the thoughts of some of them probably turned to Christmas shopping and their preparations for the Christmas season which was soon to be upon them. But they knew that, once the Christmas and New Year festivities were over, they would need to get down to the work of planning how this new building when finished could be turned into the caring home for the twenty one or so elderly people who would be living there. They realised, too, that getting that preparation right was just as important as having a suitable building.

Those preparations could be seen as in two parts. The first was to plan how to equip and furnish the building for its purpose and provide it with all necessary amenities for both residents and staff. The second was to organise the running and use of the Home once it was ready, this including the staffing and initial occupation. Few, if any, of the committee members had had experience in residential care home management. However, again they were helped through new people with relevant expertise joining the team

Two ladies who were of great assistance in the furnishing were Shirley Blabey and Janet Thomas. Shirley was an occupational therapist from America then living at Chislehurst for a short period. She and her husband Eugene were both interested in the project and Eugene came on to the management committee for a while. Their few years in Bromley were timely in that it enabled them to make a real contribution to this project. Shirley conscientiously considered the kind of chairs, tables and, where necessary, beds suitable for elderly residents, studied catalogues, made recommendations and finally ordered all these items.

She shared this task with Janet, a lady with artistic bent, who also advised on décor, curtains, etc.

Two other people who joined the development committee at the time were Rev Harold Brooker and Margaret Earp. Harold had been involved previously in the running of 'The Elms', a small home for elderly people run by churches in Peckham and Dulwich. His experience proved a great help when planning the running of Beechmore, particularly in relation to staffing. Harold later became Chaplain of Beechmore but sadly died a few years later. Later on, his wife, Dorothy, became a Beechmore resident and ended her life there. Harold's influence comes up further in the story, too, and the main Brooker lounge at Beechmore is named after them.

Margaret was a State Registered Nurse who for some years had been Matron of Derwent House, a Mission Care home in Chislehurst. She helped considerably in relation to potential needs of residents and on decisions relating to equipment like aids and hoists as well as in the recruitment of suitable staff.

Joyce Wigner and Rose Holly, two people with catering experience, looked at all the kitchen equipment and cooking utensils needed as well as the crockery and cutlery.

Reg Knight again designed the garden layout. Sadly he died before the Home was opened but his plans were followed and this helped to make the garden an attractive amenity for residents.

By the time building work had started, the Registered Homes Act had become law and its accompanying regulations were being published. These had to be closely observed if Beechmore was going to be registered and without registration no potential resident could be admitted. Wisely, contact had been made with the Social Services Inspection Officer during earlier planning and this continued. She was helpful and took an interest in the project. This made it possible to consult with her in advance on the application of the Act and its Regulations, much of which was almost as new to her as to ourselves.

So the work of preparation and planning was spread among a small group or groups of people, each of which took responsibility for different aspects of the new Home with the development committee coordinating. Organising the staffing and allocating places to residents were major tasks of two separate working groups and their work is described in later chapters. Implementing the decisions made on furniture, equipment, and fitting out was no mean task. Apart from placing the orders, they could not be carried out, of course, until the building had been completed and released by the contractors.

The builders may have been hoping for practical completion before Christmas but, in the event, the completed building was not handed over to the client until 3 February. The committee was optimistically planning for an opening of the Home by the end of March. This allowed about seven or eight weeks to get the building ready for occupation and have all the operating arrangements in place.

The builders left the site on 3 February, of course, but Reg Garthwaite stayed and proved his worth again as the key man in charge of the building during that seven week period. Not only he did he take care of the empty building, keep it warm, test all its amenities and discover any problems, he was able to co-ordinate the delivery and installation of equipment, furniture, etc. This he did with a cheerfulness and enthusiasm which proved infectious and became shared by the various people directly involved at that crucial time.

Some of the atmosphere during those few weeks is perhaps gained from reading the minutes of the development committee meeting on Friday evening 28 February. Here there are references to problems over door-closing devices, front door entry-phone control, hand dryers, a pump for the dishwasher, position of overflows, shower curtain rails and the Scots pine tree in the garden! Presumably these and various other problems were all resolved shortly afterwards as plans proceeded for the opening of the home towards the end of March and the admission of the first residents. But before we describe that happy event, it is important to see how the major task of staffing the Home was resolved and how the places for residents were filled.

Chapter 13
Recruiting the Staff

It is a truism to point out how important to any establishment is the quality of the staff and their attitude to the work and to other people. Sometimes our choice of shop or bank is influenced as much by the way we are treated by their staff as by their marketing. If this is so in a business establishment, how much more does it apply to an enterprise the sole object of which is to serve and care for people who are vulnerable and dependant upon them? If those people are to feel secure and comfortable in their new environment, they need to have complete confidence in those who are caring for them and be able to believe that they have their welfare at heart. Rightly or wrongly, they look for an even higher standard of 'tender loving care' when the home is run by a voluntary Christian organisation.

The small subcommittee to whom the task of finding the staff to run the home was allocated were well aware of this. They knew that the success of the whole project depended greatly on their work. However good the building turned out to be and however well equipped and furnished it was, unless the Home could be run by committed, caring and adequately qualified staff, the project would be seen as a disappointment. If prayer was needed for any aspect of the development, it was certainly this and the three members of that subcommittee fully understood this.

Earlier in the planning much thought had been given to the nature and number of the staff that would be required and information had been gained through contact with Abbeyfield and other organisations now running similar homes. A form of staff structure had been discussed, costed and agreed and job descriptions produced. Local Authority Guidelines as to the staff required to be on duty by day and night had to be complied with although these were soon seen as a minimum if the home was to be run smoothly. Staff costs were expected to absorb around 75% of total running costs and were, therefore, a major factor in the operating cost budget which it was necessary to keep within the projected fee income - then assumed to be £120 per week per resident, the DSS ceiling for residential care. So, although there was no intention to expect staff to work below current market rates, the subcommittee were hardly in a position to offer great financial incentives in their recruitment. It was also fairly obvious that there would need to be some reliance upon voluntary assistance for some desirable but not essential services.

Recruiting senior staff who shared the Christian ethos and objectives of Cedarmore was deemed to be of paramount importance as this would set the tone for the Home as a whole. The most important posts to fill, of course, were those of Head of Home and her Deputy and recruitment for these started in September 1985. As the new building would incorporate two small staff flats, it was possible to advertise nationwide as well as locally for these posts, using both 'The Lady', Nursing Times and one or two national Christian journals. The response was quite good and short lists of likely candidates were soon compiled and several people interviewed.

It was encouraging again how the right persons for these two posts seemed to come along and how the appointments were agreed without controversy. There were several interesting applications for the Head of Home position but the subcommittee had little difficulty in recommending one of the applicants, Christine Benison, for this post. Christine was a State Registered Nurse with many years experience in senior positions in residential homes and in the NHS. She warmed to the Beechmore project and seemed to be just the person to get the Home started, organise the staff and establish right procedures for the care of residents. She was approaching retirement age and it was obvious that she would not want to stay in the post for very long. Nevertheless, this did not seem a disadvantage as it would give Beechmore the benefit of her considerable expertise and experience in its early days and set a pattern for the future. In the event, this is precisely what happened. She stayed for barely 18 months but in that time did a great deal for the

Home, gave confidence to the new residents and was a blessing to the project. Christine was able to take up the appointment on 3rd February and was thus able to help in the preparations for the opening of the Home and be involved in nearly all the other staff appointments.

Finding the right Deputy Head did not come quite so easily. Several qualified people were interviewed but, for differing reasons, none seemed quite right for the job. As the subcommittee was reviewing the position after the last of those interviews, it occurred to one of its members to look through the unsuccessful applications for the Head of Home position. One of these was from a nurse in Harrogate whose interesting application had attracted attention at the time but did not seem to quite justify bringing her all way down to Bromley for interview. The thought came to them to enquire as to whether that person would be interested in applying for the Deputy position - a post which she was then holding in a Social Services home in Yorkshire. When she was spoken to on the telephone the following day, her response was not discouraging. There was further positive telephone discussion a day or two later and arrangements were made for her to come down for an interview with the subcommittee and with Christine Benison and to see the project. This all went very satisfactorily and there was little difficulty afterwards in reaching unanimity over offering her the Deputy Head of Home position. Happily, she was able to accept this and shared with us the feeling that in this appointment our prayers were again being answered. That lady was Ann Kemavor who later succeeded Christine as Head of Home and made a remarkable and enduring contribution to the Beechmore project, to which we shall refer later.

There were, of course, many other appointments to be made. As well as care staff, the Home needed catering and domestic staff, a secretary/clerk and a handyman. Somehow, during that period of around eight weeks in February and March, suitable people were found to fill all these posts. There had been some advertising and news of the project had certainly reached the local community and been spread through local churches. As a consequence, unexpected applications to join the staff were received from a number of local people, including one or two nurses and several experienced carers. With their years of experience it was not difficult for Christine, Margaret and Harold to discover the quality and suitability of the people concerned and within a very short time a capable and committed team of senior and assistant carers were brought together for the running of the Home. Amongst those joining Beechmore at that time were Mary Harding, Barbara Saunders, Diane Emmins, Pat McQueen and, a little later, Barbara Seiersen, for most of whom this was the beginning of a long and valuable association with the work of Cedarmore.

One interesting care assistant appointment was that of Lesley who came from Castleford in Yorkshire. Lesley was only 18 at the time and, although without any care work experience, she had heard about the project and applied to be considered for one of the vacancies. The Committee was impressed by her letter and, as Ann Kemavor had not yet moved down from Yorkshire, they asked her to interview Lesley there. Ann took to Lesley and saw her potential. She suggested that with some initial training and work under supervision, she would make a good care assistant. This advice was accepted and Lesley became one of the most helpful and popular of all the Beechmore care assistants. Soon she met Jonathan at one of the local churches and when they were married at Castleford a few years later, nearly half the Beechmore staff and not a few committee members found their way up to Yorkshire for the wedding!

Finding a cook or chef to take responsibility for all the catering was not expected to be easy. Providing suitable and enjoyable meals for the residents would always be a vital part of the care programme. If these were inadequate, unpalatable or just uninteresting, the overall welfare and contentment of residents would be impaired. It was another unexpected blessing, therefore, when Rose Holly from Elmstead Church who had helped considerably in decisions on the kitchen and general catering equipment agreed to join the staff and become its first Cook in Charge. Rose was a brilliant cook and organised the catering provision with imagination, efficiency, and even economy. All were very sorry when she had to leave the job four years later on moving away from the district. One of those who joined Rose's catering team at the time as a kitchen assistant was Helen who liked the environment so much that she was still working there 22 years later in 2008!

Staff to do the daily cleaning and run the laundry were recruited also. Amongst these was Jean whose standard was so high and commitment so reliable that after a short time she was given overall responsibility for the domestic work - a position she held for nearly fifteen years. She too loved being part of the Beechmore family and can still be seen helping there in a smaller way today.

Although most of Cedarmore administration work was still being carried out voluntarily, it was recognised in the early days of planning that Beechmore would need to employ a capable person to look after the day to day office work, including particularly management of the payroll, payment of invoices and collection of fees. A retired bookkeeper or accountant would be the kind of person to do this. And so it proved. One who had heard of the project through Harold was Bert Mercer who had just retired from an accountant position and was looking for some 'part-time' work where he could usefully employ his skills. The project appealed to him and he seemed just right for Beechmore. Again, so it turned out and Bert became a valuable and trusted member of the team - appreciated by staff and residents alike. When he retired from this position seven years later, he continued to attend the office one or two days a week to serve voluntarily in a receptionist capacity.

And the handyman/maintenance worker? Well, later in the year Henry came along and did this job thoroughly for several years. When he had to retire Ted joined the team and made an equally helpful and important contribution to the life of the Home. But in those early months Reg was still around keeping an eye on the building and its plant and equipment, ensuring the heating was adequate, the water not too hot and the lift working satisfactorily! What a gift he, too, was to Beechmore in those early days.

So, when the management committee met on 27 February it was possible to report that staff recruitment was proceeding satisfactorily and on 20 March, the only outstanding requirements were for a week-end cook and one care assistant for one night a week - gaps which were able to be filled temporarily until adequately covered.

Thus, the work of this subcommittee also had been greatly blessed. Not only did it become possible to present a full establishment to justify the opening of the Home a few days later, but the result of that work was to bring together a team of lovely people committed to helping to make the project a great success. How they were successful in this and how this affected the lives of the elderly folk whom they came to serve is revealed in our later chapters.

Yes, and volunteers came along too! From the start, reliance on volunteers was going to be needed to have someone in the office to receive visitors, answer the telephone, etc and relieve staff in this way. As mentioned earlier, one of the first persons to help in this way was Ken Wallace and others soon joined him, so much so that this position is still covered by voluntary helpers almost every week day. Over the years their presence in the front office has been of immense value. Unexpectedly too in those early years most of the gardening work was done by a volunteer. John Nichols who had recently retired from British Telecom and loved gardening took responsibility for planting and maintaining the garden and did a wonderful job on this to the delight of residents, even involving some of them in his plant decisions. Another voluntary service was the weekly trolley shop which Peggy Sanders set up and provided for nearly ten years - a service which others have continued to this day. Others offered to provide transport for hospital appointments, outings, etc and in running activities. Voluntary support in all these ways was welcomed by staff and an encouragement to them.

Chapter 14
The First Residents

From the start of the planning for this project Cedarmore had made clear that its objective was to provide 'extra care' for elderly men and women who were no longer able to provide adequately for themselves in their own homes or in sheltered accommodation. It was the intention also that priority in allocation of places should be given to residents of either of the sheltered schemes who were in that situation. That situation, after all, was one of the concerns which led to the adoption of the project.

One objective, too, had been to provide such care and support within 'an unobtrusive Christian environment'. This did not mean, of course, that every resident had to be a Church member, or a practising Christian, but it was thought important that all prospective residents should be aware of this aspect of the Home. It was interesting to discover later that one or two of the residents who did not regard themselves as practising Christians considered this to be a 'plus point' as, in their view, it contributed to the quality of care!

There was one other important factor which had to be borne in mind when considering who were to occupy the places in the new Home. The legislative framework for care homes which had been considerably strengthened by the 1984 Registered Homes Act, made a strong distinction between nursing homes and residential care homes. Housing Corporation funding terms and other considerations meant that Beechmore had to be a residential care home and not a nursing home. The distinction between nursing and residential care is not always as clear as it might be - the precise dividing line is sometimes blurred - but there was no doubt that Beechmore's status as a residential care home would prevent it from admitting some needy elderly people who had acute disabilities or whose condition had deteriorated to such a degree that they could only be appropriately cared for in a nursing home. It was desirable that most residents should be ambulant on admission although even amongst the very first residents there were three who were permanently in wheelchairs. Notwithstanding this restriction on admission, from the beginning it was a declared intention to endeavor to care for residents at the Home until the end of their lives, if at all possible. That has not always been possible, of course. Some have died in hospital and a few have had to be transferred to nursing homes but over the past twenty years by far the majority of residents have been able to end their lives peacefully in the Home under the care of Beechmore staff, as they have wished.

One factor which the subcommittee did not have to consider was the financial means of the applicants. As with places in the sheltered schemes, the policy was to allocate these on the basis of need and not take into account the financial circumstances of the applicant. This has remained Cedarmore policy up to the present day although it was perhaps easier to apply that policy then than it has been at times in more recent years. At that time, and until the Community Care legislation came into operation in 1993, residents who were unable to meet the residential care fees out of their income, and had little capital, were able to have their State Pension supplemented through the DSS so as to fully cover the fee, (and also leave a little 'pocket money'!). Nor was it then necessary for Social Services to assess that applicant's need for residential care before granting this supplement, as, perhaps understandably, it has been since 1993.

The assessment of need was left to the provider. In a sense, therefore, this simplified the allocation decisions and, as it turned out, around half of the early residents had their fees supplemented through DSS, with the other half fully self-funding. Although it was important for Bert in the office to know which residents were DSS supported and which were not, this information was kept confidential and not generally known by other residents or care staff. True, there was then a 'ceiling' up to which DSS would supplement the fees which could bring budgeting problems from time to time but this was not a factor which those allocating the places were allowed in any way to take into account.

So, as the admissions subcommittee set about its work of deciding who should be offered the 22 places which would become available in the new development, they had these considerations much in mind.

Their first task was to ascertain from the Wardens which residents in Cedarmore Court or Southmore Court needed and wanted to transfer to Beechmore and to consider those cases. This was not too difficult and, after the visits and family discussions, eight of the 22 places were allocated in that way - four from each scheme.

In the previous chapter we referred to the early publicity given to the project locally having the effect of attracting applications from potential staff. Not unexpectedly, the same thing happened in relation to potential residents. From early 1985 onwards enquiries started to come in from elderly people seeing a future need for this kind of care or from their relatives and from social workers and Church pastors or pastoral workers. In September 1985, Margaret, Muriel and others started to go through the completed application forms and try to decide which cases to follow up with a personal visit and, in most cases, a family discussion. Whilst greatness of need was a major factor, they were conscious of the importance of having a balance of need amongst this first group of residents, if staff were to be able to cope adequately. By the end of the year, most applicants had been visited and a list of the recommended first residents had been drawn up and was ready for discussion with the Head of Home on her arrival. It was perhaps a sign of Christine Benison's confidence and professional experience that, although she made contact with all these people, she did not choose to amend any of the recommendations and was happy to take over from the start what was no mean responsibility - the full care of this group of frail elderly people with a mixture of needs, tastes and prejudices. And, with the help of her staff, she did it well.

So, for those 22 prospective residents and their families, as well as the Head of Home and Beechmore helpers, March was a busy month. With an opening by the end of the month confidently predicted, agreements had to be signed, information on individual needs assembled, decisions made on the small items of furniture which residents could bring, telephone connections ordered, etc and financial arrangements put in place. Where DSS help was going to be needed with fee payment, Brian with his usual patience and his banking experience, again came to the rescue and quietly pointed people in the right direction, sometimes filling up forms for them.

They were an interesting group of elderly people, as we shall discover later. Not unusual, there were only three men amongst them. There was one married couple. The average age was 85, perhaps surprisingly low in retrospect. Twenty or so years later when many of us have reached that age with little health impediment, it seems an early average age for residential care. But this just illustrates some of the demographic change even during that short period - at the turn of the century the average age of the residents would have been around 90! This still meant that most were people who had been through two world wars and experienced some of the hardship and poverty in the years surrounding them. Some had been widowed through them. To Christine and her team and to all those behind the project, there was little doubt that these twenty two people were in need of the extra care which Beechmore was promising to give. By the middle of the month, most had been allocated rooms and given provisional entry dates but there was still one major hurdle as the next chapter will reveal

Chapter 15
Now We Can Open

It was the day preceding the first day of Spring 1986 when, at around 10 am on that pleasant Thursday morning, the attractive London Borough of Bromley Homes Registration Officer arrived at the new premises, by then known as Beechmore Court, to see whether it could be registered and opened as the residential care home for which it was intended. Christine and Ann were expecting her arrival and were both there waiting to escort her round the building, show her its equipment and demonstrate their readiness to open the doors to those 22 people who were to be its first residents. Val Hughes was not a complete stranger to the project. She had been consulted earlier on at various stages of the planning process and had always been friendly and helpful and, indeed, interested in the project. But she was the first Bromley Registration Officer to be appointed under the 1984 Registered Homes Act and took her responsibilities seriously and could not be expected to compromise on any inadequacy in the care or accommodation provision. She inspected the whole building thoroughly, examining and testing equipment like the lift, hoists, fire alarm and call system, even testing the temperature of the hot water. She looked at the kitchen and catering provision and the cleaning and laundry arrangements and discussed the staff rotas and supervision arrangements with Christine and Ann. This was probably the first new home which she had had to inspect and she seemed well pleased with what she found. She made a few suggestions but saw nothing to prevent her authorising the issue of a Registration Certificate or delay the opening of the Home.

Although such registration was expected, and indeed had been assumed as forthcoming in the staffing and resident admission arrangements, it could not be taken for granted. It was a great relief when the certificate was issued the following day. This perhaps demonstrated the thoroughness of the planning which had taken place during the preceding months. Val, in fact, attended the informal opening of the Home on the Saturday and retained an interest in it during the several subsequent years whilst she held this post. Both Christine and Ann found her helpful and consulted with her on various occasions as situations arose. As on numerous other occasions in Cedarmore work, this demonstrated the value of good relations with representatives of the Authorities. Respecting their essential role and endeavoring to work with them has nearly always proved far more profitable than a confrontational attitude which some in the voluntary sector may be inclined to adopt.

With all the optimism and faith which seems to have surrounded this project from the start, an unofficial opening of the Home was planned for Saturday afternoon 22 March and supporters of the project, committee members, staff and relatives of some of the prospective residents, as well as Roger Sims, still the local MP and a good friend of Cedarmore, and one or two of the local Church ministers, were invited. All crowded into the large new lounge, most standing, whilst Donald Cranefield conducted a short service of thanksgiving and dedication of the new building. Both Roger and Donald had taken part in the opening of Southmore Court and in the Stone laying for this building and were thus able to share with us all in the joy and excitement of the occasion.

It was not intended quite as a celebration. That was expected to take place later at an Official Opening when the Home was full. On this day, most were conscious that there was still plenty of work to be done during the next few weeks as residents would arrive and staff settle in. Yet, as Harold introduced Christine and Ann and a number of the new staff to us and we shared the refreshments prepared in the new kitchen and, as folk saw the new building and all its amenities for the first time, there was a great sense of satisfaction and achievement. More so, too, a feeling of thanksgiving that this final stage had been reached in a quite remarkable way, feelings perhaps better expressed in the hymn sung together 'Now thank we all our God with hearts and hands and voices'.

With staff now in place, over the following fortnight from the Monday onwards, the new residents started to arrive, one or two each day. Relatives and friends, as well as the staff, helped them to settle in and adapt to the new environment. Reg Garthwaite was at hand to help with some of the practical problems. Most brought some of their own furniture, a chair or two, a table or bookcase, a radio or television - one or two even their own beds - provided they met safety regulations. Pictures and photographs began to appear on walls and rooms began to reflect some of the characters of the residents concerned or reminders of their past lives. By 7 April, barely a fortnight from the unofficial opening, the Head of Home could report that every permanent room was occupied and someone would be coming into the respite care room shortly.

Staff were also settling in, getting to know each other and the residents. The quality of the staff which had come together was soon evident and a sense of loyalty and belonging soon spread among them - due no little to the example in commitment and enthusiasm set by both Christine and Ann. Although residents had freedom to stay in their own rooms as much as they wanted, they were expected to come down for lunch and for the evening meal and they were encouraged to come down to the lounge for morning coffee and afternoon tea and a few activities, as much as possible. This helped them to get to know one another and, within a very short time, most seemed pleased to be there and a small community had emerged.

The Official Opening was held on a Saturday afternoon in July, with Rev Norman Wright, who had been closely involved in the Romford project referred to earlier, and was now President of the Baptist Union, performing the ceremony. This was a happy and fairly informal occasion with residents and staff participating and some residents' families and supporters attending. By then, the project really felt completed and the fruit of all the endeavours apparent for all to see.

But would this happy situation remain and could the enthusiasm and commitment of those early months be retained, as time went on and there were inevitably problems to be resolved and unexpected situations to be faced. This is the subject of the next chapter.

Chapter 16
Beechmore - the Early Years

The value and success of any enterprise must be judged largely by the degree of client satisfaction which it brings. There may be others factors to take into account in a project like Beechmore but a most, if not the most, important criteria in judging its success has to be as to how secure and contented its residents feel in their new environment. Providing such contentment in this kind of situation is not so easily achieved. Most elderly folk do not relish the idea of moving into a residential care or nursing home. When it becomes necessary, they do so with a degree of foreboding and resignation. They may welcome the care that they will receive and freedom from daily chores which have become burdensome and the end of a loneliness which for some has been hard to endure. But most are reluctant to leave the place which has been their home for many years and many of the memories and things which surround it. In such circumstances, to provide a sense of security, comfort and well-being for those people in such new environment at this last stage of their lives is no mean achievement - and a great credit to the supervisors and staff of any residential care or nursing home concerned.

Without exaggeration and if residents themselves and their families are to be believed, it is probably fair to claim that that sense of security and contentment has been achieved for the majority of Beechmore residents throughout most of the twenty years or so since it was opened. There have been a few exceptions and there are always some who are unable to come to terms with having to leave their own homes - but they seem to have been a small minority. During those early years of Beechmore, and indeed later, it was the knowledge of this achievement and the blessing which the Home seemed to bring to the majority of its residents at this time of need in their lives which, to all those involved and to the staff of the Home, made all the effort which had gone into the project seem so much worth while. And what were the secrets of this?

One reason, of course, was the quality and commitment of the staff which had been assembled. On the whole they, too, were a contented staff who quickly learned to work together and enjoyed their working environment. As with nurses in hospitals, their sense of humour helped, particularly with some of the less pleasant duties. The tone, of course, was set by the Head of Home and her Deputy. Both believed in a disciplined high standard of care and both believed in 'hands on' management, teaching by example and not being afraid of doing routine chores themselves when this was necessary. They worked well together and, in a sense, they complemented each other. Christine was in some ways like a good old fashioned hospital matron - but approachable and not a 'battle axe' in any way. She was efficient and caring with an interest in the health and welfare of each resident and in ensuring staff adhered to proper care procedures. Ann, though through her early nursing training likewise committed to high standards of care, was particularly interested in the quality of life of the residents. She was keen to encourage activities for them and help them to continue to take an interest in life outside the Home. Christine gave her a free hand in this and some interesting activities took place.

When Christine retired in June 1987, after two farewell parties and some sadness, Ann was promoted to Head of Home in her place. Although her style was quite different, she was happy to build on the disciplined care programme which her predecessor had created and continued with her holistic approach to the welfare of residents. It proved difficult to recruit a new Deputy Head of Home and instead two senior care assistants, Mary Harding and Barbara Saunders, were appointed Assistant Heads of Home. So continued the practice, which has been repeated throughout the Cedarmore organisation on several occasions since, of promoting good, known staff to fill vacancies in supervisory positions. Mary and Barbara were both committed to the well-being of the residents and were part of the Cedarmore family for many years. When, a few years later, Mary left Beechmore to take over as Warden at Cedarmore Court, her place was taken by another senior care assistant, Barbara Seiersen, who too became a loved and trusted member of the team for many years. Barbara Saunders, even to this day although now 'retired', still helps occasionally with relief supervisory duties - having served there for over 20 years!

A great achievement of these leaders was to instill that sense of mission and commitment into the staff upon whom they were so dependant. In many of the staff this was there already. In others it had to be developed - mostly by example. Inevitably a few of the original staff left for various reasons, but others took their place, most sharing the ethos of the Home. These included Edna and her two daughters who for several years covered much of the night duty and who had the great gift of making residents laugh whilst attending to their personal needs. The need for some training to help improve performance and understand the needs of residents was soon recognised, Ann herself leading some training periods and inviting specialists in for others.

Another reason for the happiness at Beechmore during those early years was undoubtedly the amount of attention it was receiving from friends and supporters of the project - from house committee members, supporting Churches and friends and relatives of residents. Perhaps this is not so unexpected - for a new project which had caught the imagination of people and in which two or three local Church communities had taken a great interest. Twenty two residents also meant twenty or so families with an elderly relative living at Beechmore, and for most of those families this meant frequent visits there and taking some interest in it. From the start, the Home encouraged visitors for residents at almost any time and allowed them freedom to stay with the resident for as long as they wished. This helped in the creation of the family and friendly atmosphere and, in the case of very frail residents, could also often be a help to staff.

It was a strong house committee, with Muriel Hyde now taking a leading part, and several, like Shirley and Janet, who had helped in the detailed planning of the project, remaining on the committee for a few months to see their work come to fruition. One person who joined this on the opening of the Home was George Marshall, who had recently moved into Cedarmore Court. George, by then over 70, had been a great sportsman and Boys Brigade leader, and took upon himself the task of providing entertainment and outside activities for residents - greatly encouraged by Ann and the staff. The house committee minutes between 1986 and 1990 give an interesting picture of some of the activities during that period - as well as outings, to which reference is made later, there were musical and quiz evenings, slide shows, a visit from the Lewisham Concert Band and from 'Bromley Barber Shop Entertainers'! During the day someone organised scrabble, crafts and a small knitting group. Most mornings over coffee a few residents gathered to do the Telegraph Crossword, Ann herself usually joining in.

Over Christmas much trouble would be taken by staff and helpers to make it a special time - with Christmas tree, decorations, etc, carol singing visits, Christmas parties, entertainment, etc. In two consecutive years, George managed to put on a Staff Pantomime - and persuaded staff and a few others to give several precious evenings rehearsing for this. These proved great fun and went down well with residents - greatly amused by the appearance of Bert and Alfred as the two ugly sisters! On Easter Monday, residents took part in Easter Bonnet displays, some, with the help of staff, showing great ingenuity in their contributions!

Outings, too, became a regular part of the activities. Initially, these were in a hired coach or private cars but the idea of having Cedarmore's own minibus soon arose. In March 1988, with funds from a legacy and other gifts, a new Renault Traffic minibus was purchased. This was soon brought into active use for outings, Church visits and other journeys. Brian Cooper, in his quiet efficient way, personally took special care of this new asset for many years. He and other volunteers became regular drivers. Four months later, he was able to report to the July House Committee meeting that the minibus had made 38 trips covering 1,265 miles. In the summer months, there was usually a weekly outing. Places visited including Chartwell, Leeds Castle, Hever Castle, Hampton Court, even Eastbourne and Folkestone

One of Ann's other ideas was to give as many residents as possible a week's holiday in a different environment and quite a few of them responded to this. In May 1987 George, Mary and Barbara took nine Beechmore residents and others from Southmore for a week's holiday at a hotel in East Cliff, Bournemouth. In both 1988 and 1989, there were two holiday parties using the minibus - one at Eastbourne led by Ann herself and a smaller one led by Barbara at Bognor. All were popular with the residents concerned and there were many wheelchair rides along the Eastbourne and Bognor promenades. In later years sadly, it became difficult to find enough residents capable of making this kind of journey or temporary adjustment.

And the spiritual life of the Home was not neglected either. From the start a service was held in the main lounge at 5 o'clock every Sunday afternoon and this has been the practice ever since, with the majority of residents attending. These were arranged by Harold in the early years and later by George with the help of Iris. Iris, now an Elenmore Court resident, bless her, has played the piano for these services for over twenty years. Most days, just before the evening meal, the Head of Home or supervisor on duty would lead a brief devotional time in the lounge. Once a month, on a weekday morning, the Chaplain would hold a Communion Service in the lounge. Both these practices have continued to this day. The Chaplain would also visit the Home from time to time, meeting residents on request and this has proved a helpful practice ever since.

How did the residents take to all this activity? They were there, after all, to be cared for - not to be entertained! Most seemed to be able to appreciate both - although there were always some too tired or too weak to enter into many of the activities. All were well cared for, as a priority - and when sickness and terminal illness came, as it did inevitably for most residents, staff did their best to give all the bedside help and comfort that was needed, as many relatives testified afterwards. Of the twelve residents lost during the first three years up to the end of 1989, six had died peacefully in their own rooms at Beechmore, five had died in hospital after very short stays there and only one had had to be transferred to a nursing home. Another surprising detail was that there was not a single loss or change of resident for a period of two years from July 1986 to June 1988 - a record which has not been reached since. This all helped to build up the sense of family and belonging -

and perhaps added to the real feeling of bereavement a few weeks later when three residents died in the one month of July 1988.

These were perhaps the 'golden years' in the life of Beechmore - years when all benefited from the freshness of the project, the enthusiasm of staff and helpers, the encouragement of local churches and the good reputation which the Home was beginning to acquire. Perhaps also, the degree of frailty amongst residents was not so great as in later years - although almost from the start there were a few residents who needed special attention.

They were in some ways a special group of old people - these 22 early residents and those taking some of their places as vacancies arose - not special by design but special in that the experiences and characters which they brought with them made Beechmore such an interesting community. Most of them could share in the fun as well as the more serious side of the Home. Staff could enjoy helping them and chatting with them whilst doing so. Most appreciated all that was being done for them. There were some interesting characters.

There was Florence, from Cedarmore Court, with the twinkle in her eye and wicked sense of humour, Eva, who had been church organist and choir leader and could not be refrained from feeding the pigeons, Ethel, whose weight was a constant problem but who loved her biscuits. Marion, now herself receiving care but never forgetting her own nursing experience and anxious to encourage the staff, Rosina very mobile in her wheelchair, Margaret, always impeccably dressed even though she had one artificial leg. Alf with his 'corny' jokes, Leslie, the perfect gentleman whose fading memory occasionally got him into difficulties, Connie, who had ridden a motor cycle in her youth and still loved to travel to Bromley and became the first resident to reach 100 and busy little Miss R - one of the very few not wanting to be known by her Christian name - a view always respected. Undoubtedly, many of the staff loved them and enjoyed caring for them.

Of course, there were problems and a few headaches. There was the one difficult resident and one or two mistakes over staff. As with any new building there were some teething problems - the ceiling heating, the artex ceilings, the hot water boiler, the guttering and a part of the roof all called for special attention. The builders had to be called back once or twice. It was a blessing to have Reg Garthwaite not too far away for most of this time as was the help and advice of John Fagg and Reg Shore - busy men who would make themselves available when there was a need.

During those first five years there were two exceptionally cold winters, temperatures in one February going down well below zero for several days, causing icicles to appear on the guttering and testing the heating system to its limits. However, there were also some warm summers and one use of the generous legacy from one of the earliest residents, Bertha Everett, was to provide a small conservatory/sun lounge looking out on to the garden. This was opened by relatives of Bertha in July 1988 and has proved a valuable amenity and hallowed spot for a number of residents ever since.

Financing the running of an enterprise like Beechmore can never be an easy task and there were concerns, of course, that it could become a burden for the Association as a whole to carry. The scheme was budgeted to be self-supporting with the fees paid by residents, many with DSS help, intended to cover all outgoings. During the second year, as unforeseen costs arose and staffing had to increase a little, this did not quite happen - but in all other years, for the first ten years or so, all running costs were covered. This was greatly helped, of course, by the high rate of occupancy, with room vacancies being very quickly filled, and by staff awareness of the need to keep running costs under control. There were times when the situation caused concern and a few headaches and fees had to be reviewed regularly. Even so, in most years it was possible to keep those fees at or very close to the DSS ceilings.

Perhaps partly because of the good reputation which Beechmore was acquiring and the continued support of churches and local people, charitable donations continued to arrive. These were a great help but never used to subsidise running costs. As with the Bertha Everett legacy, they would be used to provide amenities, equipment and improvements to the Home to benefit residents and staff. Annual events like the Summer and Christmas Fayres, useful social events in themselves, also brought in funds which were usually used to improve amenities. Beechmore benefited considerably from such extra financial help - as it still does to-day.

It was not really surprising that the waiting list for places at Beechmore began to grow. Success can often bring its own problems. There were 15 names left on that list when the first residents were admitted. By July 1988 this had grown to 47 and the Committee began to think of ways of providing more rooms.

An opportunity to do this arose later that year when part of the grounds of the Pinewood Nursing Home behind Beechmore was acquired by developers for new housing. This temporarily provided a rear access to the property and encouraged the idea of a small extension at that end of the building, still within the Beechmore grounds. Derek quickly produced a simple but attractive plan for a two storey extension which provided four additional rooms, this time each with spacious en suite toilets, as well as some additional facilities. Obtaining planning consent for this did not prove difficult but over £100,000 funding was required. The Housing Corporation again proved helpful and soon agreed in principle to provide 60% of the funds required, if Cedarmore found the rest by a combination of bank loan and charitable funding. A Loan facility with National Westminster Bank was negotiated and an Appeal soon went out to various Trusts and supporters, led again by Andrew and Elizabeth. There were some encouraging responses and a few interesting fundraising events took place. Ralph organised a sponsored walk in which quite a few staff took part which raised £1,700. Roger laid on a Church concert which provided another £450.

The work went out to tender and building work started in the Spring of 1989 and was completed by September. The extension was officially opened by Helen Dunwell of the Tudor Trust in October. Four new residents were then able to move into these special rooms. The eventual total cost of the extension with furnishings, etc was around £130,000, towards which the Housing Corporation provided £79,000. The remaining £51,000 came from charitable grants and donations, making it unnecessary to take up any of the loan facility. How blessed was Cedarmore - once again.

A year later it was possible to acquire a house for staff accommodation nearby and the Head of Home was able to occupy part of this. This enabled the small part of the Beechmore building where the staff flat had been, to be converted into two more resident rooms, again with en suite toilets. This had the effect of bringing the number of residents up to 28, with one of the rooms used for respite care.

Was the project now complete? One might have thought so. But around 1988, a light cloud began to appear on the Beechmore horizon, a cloud which caused considerable concern to Ann and her caring colleagues and darkened in the succeeding years. The name of that cloud was dementia. Like many clouds, this one had a silver lining. How that concern was met and faced up to is another important phase in the Cedarmore story and the subject of the following chapters.

PART IV
THE DEMENTIA
CHALLENGE

Chapter 17
The Problem

A degree of dementia in some older people towards the end of their lives is, of course, no new problem. It has always existed and nearly always sooner or later has meant a heavy burden to be carried by both the sufferer and the relative or other person caring for them. What has changed, of course, is the public perception of the illness and our treatment of it. Indeed it is probably true to say that, in both of these ways, there has been change even during the past twenty years since Beechmore Court was opened. That change probably reflects the increasing incidence of Alzheimer's disease or some other form of dementia in older people as they are living longer and the publicity now being given to it. Public awareness of the illness and the need for proper care for its sufferers has been greatly enhanced by the work of the Alzheimer's Society and through publicity given in the media to incidences of it, not least in some well known people such as Ronald Reagan, Iris Murdoch and Terry Pratchett. Most people in England should now know a little about Alzheimer's and indeed there must be few who haven't heard of or come across someone suffering from it.

Yet it seems that, when Beechmore Court was opened in 1986, that change in the public perception of dementia and in the understanding of the special care needs of those suffering from it was only beginning to happen. It may have been well advanced among the professionals and academics and in the United States and some parts of Europe but ordinary British people still seemed to shy away from the subject or want to hide its existence. We had stopped putting dementia sufferers in mental hospitals or hospital psychiatric wards but many were being placed in ordinary residential care or nursing homes alongside physically frail or disabled people or with people suffering from other mental illnesses. Many families were still carrying the burden of caring at home for a spouse or parent with dementia, with limited support from the outside world. Some people were still referring to the condition as 'senile dementia', a somewhat derogatory term which seemed to have some stigma attached to it. Nowadays we tend to use the term 'Alzheimer's' to cover most dementia although it is only one form of the disease, albeit the most prevalent - and this does seem to have taken away most of the stigma. Yet the incidence of dementia was and is increasing. Around 1990, it was believed that one in ten people in the United Kingdom over 85 were likely to be suffering from dementia with a higher proportion still amongst those over 90. Those proportions are now believed to be higher although, thanks to the work of the Alzheimer's Society and others, much more is now known as to the cause of the illness and ways of impeding its development.

When consideration was being given as to who were to be the first residents of Beechmore Court there was a general understanding as to the kind of need which the Home would meet. As the original brochure said, the Home was for 'elderly men and women who are no longer able to provide adequately for themselves in their own homes or in sheltered accommodation'. It was reluctantly accepted that it would not be possible to admit someone who from the beginning needed continuous nursing care even though that need might arise for some residents later. Little thought appears to have been given, however, as to whether there would be any place for an elderly person perhaps in the early stages of dementia. It was recognised that a degree of 'confusion' in some residents was bound to arise eventually and this was assumed to be something which could be contained and managed as an inevitable feature of any residential care home for elderly people. This was probably the general view at the time. As it happened, none of the first twenty two residents appeared to suffer from dementia in any form. Two of these later became what would then have been described as 'mentally confused' but this was accepted as unsurprising and presented no real problem.

Problems began to arise two years later, however, as two or three new residents arrived, mainly folk transferred from one of the sheltered schemes. The 'confusion' of those residents had made it difficult for them to cope within their sheltered housing environment and the Wardens, and the residents' families, understandably saw a transfer to Beechmore as the solution to their problem. Beechmore, after all, was for those for whom sheltered housing was inadequate and Ann and her staff accepted the transfer as part of their responsibility and welcomed these needy people into the Beechmore family. This was the beginning of a situation which would undoubtedly have arisen at some time given the nature of the home. It is perhaps worth referring in some detail to one or two of these residents, most of whom were later diagnosed as suffering from dementia - although the symptoms could not have been more different in each case.

Doris was a single lady in her late eighties who had lived happily at Cedarmore Court for the previous three or four years. She was a gentle soul who was liked by everyone - including the Beechmore cat that always chose her bed when he wanted a nap! She lived completely in a world of her own, largely oblivious of the world around her, remembering little of it or of the daily routine. She had a very deep but simple faith and loved to pray. She would become frightened, however, if something unusual happened and needed assurance and comforting at such times.

Florrie and her husband had lived in the larger flat at Southmore Court for several years. Her husband had died recently and during his last year had suffered from what was clearly some form of dementia. This had taken its toll on her and she now needed being taken care of. She soon developed a form of dementia herself which prevented her from staying in one situation for any length of time. She became a 'wanderer' in the home, recalling memories of her early days and asking to be taken home to her mother. At time she was quite distressed which was painful to observe.

Another new resident around the same time was Betty, a widowed lady who had been living with relatives in the area who had found it difficult to cope. Prior to her bereavement she had lived at Ilford in Essex. Her condition was erratic and much of the time she behaved rationally. She too was active physically and wanted to go out. Ann's policy was always to encourage activity on the part of residents and

Betty's need was often met by a member of staff taking her for a short walk 'round the block'. On one occasion, however, Betty found her own way out, probably as a visitor was entering the building, and it was twenty minutes or so before her absence was noticed.

When it was realised that she had left the building, a search party of staff and friends were summoned and literally scoured the neighborhood, including the Jubilee Park fields. Her relatives and the Police were informed and it was thought she might have gone to London. Well into the summer evening, when there was growing anxiety and prayers at Beechmore, her Bickley relatives received a telephone call from neighbors of Betty's old home at Ilford to say that they had seen her walking past the house. Needless to say, she was fetched immediately and returned, apparently none the worse for her adventure. How she found her way from Bickley to Ilford was never known but the conclusion was that she had taken a bus to Woolwich, crossed the river by ferry and caught another bus to Ilford - a journey which she had undertaken many times in the past. Needless to say, much discussion at Beechmore followed!

A fourth, also very different, resident was Leslie - a widower, a lovely man and the perfect gentleman. He was probably in the early stages of Alzheimer's, suffering mainly from short term memory loss. He had settled well at Beechmore. He had been a keen bowls player and, to help maintain his interest, Ann would often drive him down the road to the local Bowling Club where he would stay for the afternoon and watch the games. She would arrange with someone at the Club to bring him back to Beechmore afterwards. One day, however, he called a taxi to take him home. When asked by the taxi driver for his destination, he gave his old address at Birchington, forty miles away! Fortunately, the taxi driver had his suspicions and made further enquiries and Leslie missed the long journey.

Beechmore staff attitude to this problem was very positive. They saw this kind of resident as just another elderly person needing their care and attention as much as the others, usually in a different way. Often though they called for a disproportionate amount of staff time and needed constant supervision. This was particularly so of Florrie. It was not possible just to meet her immediate need and then leave to attend to the needs of another resident. Even so, there was no complaint from staff over her presence in the Home - rather there was great sympathy for her condition.

The attitude of other residents was not quite so straightforward. Most were genuinely sympathetic and concerned for the welfare of these residents. They were also thankful that old age had not brought them that kind of problem - and that they themselves still 'had their marbles'. But there were one or two who began to resent the presence of Florrie and Betty and were unable to hide their feelings. This is understandable in a way as it can be no fun having to share a meal table with someone who often forgets when to use the knife, fork or spoon or whether to put salt or sugar into their tea! They could also see these residents receiving more attention than themselves. The sad thing was that Florrie and Betty were not immune to sensing an atmosphere and they began to realise that their presence was not wanted by some residents and this added to their unhappiness.

This situation particularly concerned Ann and several of her colleagues and they began to look for ways of managing the situation and think how best to care for the dementia sufferers. Ann herself took a personal interest in the welfare of Florrie and sought to understand the dementia which was causing her such distress. She had had little previous experience of dementia in old people and so began to read books on the subject, even taking a university correspondence course on it. She would discuss some of her findings with colleagues and soon became convinced that dementia residents needed a special kind of care, different from that needed for physically frail residents, and that they could be best cared for in a separate environment and in a small family-like setting. She learned of a few other places where this policy had been adopted successfully and began to share her conviction with other staff and helpers.

Ann shared this opinion with house committee members and others and it soon became an accepted view that dementia residents would be better cared for separately from physically frail residents. In retrospect, perhaps, it is surprising that the reaction of some was not to suggest that Beechmore should then concentrate only on caring for physically frail elderly people and leave dementia care to others. This was not the reaction. Rather, the unanimous conclusion seemed to be that Beechmore must try to find a way to put that policy into practice. That conclusion may have been influenced to some extent by the fact that, so far as they were aware, there was no such specific provision in the area. More positively though, influenced by Ann's infectious enthusiasm, they began to see this as a new challenge for Cedarmore - to extend their Christian caring ministry to bring in some of the most vulnerable of elderly people - those for whom old age had sadly brought mental confusion, memory loss and indeed dementia.

But it was one thing to take up that challenge and a brave thing to do so. It was another to find a way of responding to it. Logically, another extension or small annex was required but how could this be provided? The Beechmore site was already well developed and it was very unlikely that permission would be given for building on it further, even were that desirable. But a separate development well away from Beechmore did not seem practicable. Yet, before the end of that year, 1989, another of those windows of opportunity, which seem to have always come at vital times in the history of Cedarmore, began to appear - almost as a confirmation that this was the right way forward. It took more than eighteen testing months of slow progress and alternating hope and disappointment for that window to open fully - but open it did eventually and this vision of Ann and her colleagues became a new project and another vital part of the work of Cedarmore. The next chapter will tell this story.

Chapter 18
A Special Care Project?

The period 1985 to 1989 had been one of those boom periods in the housing market when properties were selling easily, prices were rising and mortgages were easy to obtain - for some perhaps a little too easily. Indeed it was not unlike the recent period up to 2007 when borrowing became so easy and some house prices reached astronomical levels. Towards the end of 1989, as happened in early 2008, the situation began to change - and the boom almost turned to bust. Mortgages became more difficult to obtain, houses became difficult to sell and prices began to fall back.

One immediate effect of this situation is to bring a slow down in new house building. Developers are reluctant to build if they foresee a problem over selling afterwards. It can also give them financial problems if they find themselves with expensive land on their hands and bank loans which they are unable to repay.

Something like this appeared to be the position at the end of 1989 with regard to the land at the back of Beechmore Court which had been acquired by a firm of builders and developers. The land represented the site of the old WRVS Pinewood Home which had had a very large garden. They had built a new care home for the WRVS on one corner of the site and had obtained planning permission for seven four bedroom detached houses on the remainder of the site, which would become Lime Close. It was the developer's possession of this site which made it logical for them to build the Beechmore four room extension referred to in Chapter 16. However, by the time that they were ready to start building, the housing slump had started and, not surprisingly, they held back from building the houses. Indeed it seems they seriously considered selling some of the building plots.

'It is an ill wind that blows no one any good' - and certainly this seemed to open a door for us. Could we acquire a site there, perhaps one or two of the plots, and erect on it the much wanted special care unit, so close to and readily accessible from Beechmore Court?

In retrospect, perhaps, it may seem surprising that Cedarmore, possibly in association with Mission Care, owners of the Homefield Nursing Home next door, did not see this as a wider opportunity and consider finding a way of acquiring the whole site for future expansion of their work. But at that time and in that period of economic slowdown, neither organisation thought in that way. Cedarmore thought only of it as an unexpected opportunity - perhaps a God-given one - to develop the special care unit so near at hand. As things turned out later, this was just as well - for it is probably unlikely that a basis for such major site acquisition would ever have been agreed.

We had met one or two of the Directors of the development company in connection with the Beechmore extension and found them to be reasonable and approachable. We found it the same in our original discussion with them on this possible site acquisition. They appeared to welcome the idea and their response was sufficiently positive to make us give attention as to how such a development could be funded. We were able to secure an early meeting with the Housing Corporation Regional Director at Croydon and explained the situation to them, Ann herself attending the meeting and speaking of the need for this unit. As expected, they gave no commitment but were sufficiently encouraging to lead us to feel that some further funding from them was possible. They advised us to submit a Bid for a funds allocation in the next financial year, 1990/91. It was clear though that, as with the Beechmore extension, there would need to be a substantial private sector or charitable funding contribution towards the cost and, such was the commitment and enthusiasm for the project, this did not seem an insurmountable obstacle. In the event, Cedarmore was again greatly blessed in this and financing the project was the relatively easier part of the exercise. Reaching agreement with the developers was another matter!

Early in 1990 it seemed appropriate to try and reach a tentative agreement with the developers on a site acquisition and we obtained site valuations, based on the existing planning consent for two alternative plots. The responsibility for negotiating this was given to Reg Shore and the writer. On making further contact with the developers, we discovered two things. Firstly, as company directors often do in this kind of situation, the nice Directors had delegated the responsibility for negotiating with us to one of their executives, whom we shall refer to as Damien. Damien was young, clever and brash and knew exactly what he wanted. He seemed determined to get for his company from this deal no less, and perhaps more, than they would have done had there been no slump in the housing market. From the first meeting we knew that the negotiations were going to be difficult. Reg and I had both been involved in quite a few negotiations over the years and yet we felt at the end that these had been one of the most difficult we had experienced. We felt that he had studied negotiating techniques even by the way he seated us in his office. His task was to present their terms - ours to accept them without question! Those negotiations lasted eighteen months and it was indeed a miracle that agreement was reached in the end. During that time, we became very familiar with the journey to their office and got to know Damien well in the process. Although we disliked some of his methods, we developed a kind of respect for his ability and for his commitment to his company's prosperity. Inevitably we clashed at times but we felt that he did develop a degree of respect for us and for our completely different outlook. At least we were able to converse amicably when different issues arose years later.

The other discovery was that the developers were no longer interested in a simple disposal of one or two of the plots so that we could have a building of our own architect's design erected upon it. They wanted a 'package deal' under which they would also design and build the new unit for us - what was then known as a 'design and build contract'. As they were builders as well as developers, this was not perhaps surprising and this would help to keep their building department occupied at a time when they were not building many houses. Indeed, design and build contracts were becoming popular in the industry and some housing associations were using them. There were dangers in doing so, however, in the sense that, unless a detailed definition of the desired unit and the standards required was agreed at the contract stage, the client was very much in the hands of the builder as to the quality of the end product. They are perhaps more suitable when there is a strong ongoing relationship between client and builder and it is not quite so necessary to define all the details.

Although we should much have preferred to acquire the site and employ our own architect, putting the work out to tender in the usual way, we did not object to combining the site acquisition with a design and build contract and understood that such arrangements were not unacceptable to the Housing Corporation. However, if Housing Corporation finance was going to be available towards this, the new building was going to have to conform to their standards as well as meet Social Services requirements for home registration purposes. The cost also needed to be kept within or close to TIC (Total Indicative Costs). A month or so later, therefore, we presented our schedule of 'Employers Requirements' to Damien and awaited his reaction. He replied later with proposals which we could not possibly accept and, after another meeting, we submitted a counter-proposal. The 'to and fro' went on until the end of the year when we at last thought that a compromise agreement had been reached and both parties agreed to instruct solicitors to work on the actual contracts. Our solicitor's interpretation of the agreement reached was not acceptable to Damien and, after one or two frustrating meetings, he instructed us to change our solicitor if we wanted the matter to proceed! Needless to say, we did nothing of the sort and the negotiations appeared to come to an end. This seemed extremely disappointing after so much effort had been put into finding a way forward. However, we wrote a letter to Damien expressing our regret and assuring him of our continued interest. Our hope had not completely evaporated and we waited.

What happened in the developer's office during the next few weeks we never knew. Favourably for us, the housing market slump had not ended and they were still not ready to build houses on the Lime Close site. A month or so later, there was a letter from Damien inviting us to a meeting with himself and his Director to consider a revised proposal. In the event most of that meeting was just with Damien and his assistant but the atmosphere was that of a meeting of old friends! We were given to understand that the Directors had reviewed the situation of the Lime Close site and concluded that, if rapid progress could be made, it would be better to do a deal with us now than consider alternative ideas. He presented us with a simple 'package deal' proposal which would meet all our requirements and satisfy the regulatory authorities, for a fixed sum. We did not discuss the proposal in any detail then but agreed to consider it carefully with our colleagues and come back to him as soon as possible. The atmosphere remained friendly and his parting remarks were to suggest that, as he was going away for three weeks holiday, we could if we wished in his absence discuss the proposal with his Director direct. We wondered afterwards whether Damien had regretted making that suggestion - for to us it was another window of opportunity and it raised new hope - if we could move quickly enough.

We were able to arrange an early meeting with several management committee colleagues to discuss this new proposal. The description of the building to be provided was surprisingly satisfactory, incorporating a number of features over which there had been discussion in the past. The only major unacceptable item was the price. The fixed sum quoted was way beyond what we knew we should be able to afford or allowed to spend. By then we had a much clearer idea as to how the project would be financed. It was also reasonable to assume that Damien himself was aware of this and expected to have to negotiate downwards. Our response, therefore, was to agree amongst ourselves what was the maximum price which Cedarmore could, and would be allowed to, pay, for the site and the building as described and to make a counter offer slightly below that figure. Although it was doubtful whether Damien himself would ever come down near to our figure, there seemed a reasonable chance that something could be agreed with the Director. We went to see him on 31 July and our counter offer, with a few small amendments to the specification, was presented to him. The meeting was very cordial and, apart from a few minor details which were subsequently settled on the telephone, a way forward was agreed. We were invited to follow this up with a formal letter to the Director confirming the agreement and a few days letter received his response. His reply dated 2 August 1991 is remarkable for its brevity and clarity 'We acknowledge receipt of your letter dated 2nd August confirming our agreement to construct a design build unit for a fixed price of £489,000 (four hundred and eighty nine thousand pounds). We have instructed our Architect to contact you immediately to finalise the minor adjustments.

After all the talking and argument, we were there at last! We took our summer holidays with thankful hearts. What Damien said when he returned from his, we never knew! Perhaps he was relieved that his Director had made the decision.

This was not quite the end of the story. In one sense it was a new beginning - but from then on it was relatively plain sailing. Both parties wanted the work to start as soon as possible. Although the building was designed by the developer's architect, we considered it necessary to have our own consultant architect to review the plans, etc. Derek Bingham had partly retired by then and another Derek began his association with Cedarmore - Derek Briscoe of Fountain Flanagan. Derek was an experienced architect who understood our needs and was able to suggest and agree several essential amendments to the plans. He also negotiated a consequential amendment to the fixed price to bring this up to £505,000, the figure to which we had to work from then on.

During the next few months planning consent for the new building was granted, the forms of site conveyance and building contract agreed and, importantly, the Housing Corporation Grant and Scheme Approval confirmed. The Grant was settled at £320,000 leaving Cedarmore to find a little over £200,000 itself if furniture and all equipment were to be covered. A major charitable trust which had developed an interest in dementia care generously offered a grant of £100,000 towards this leaving Andrew and Elizabeth the task of raising the remaining £100,000. A Bank Loan was negotiated in case this should be needed. It was February 1992 before contracts were finally exchanged and on 18th March the builders started work on the site, expecting to finish before the end of the year. There was now no turning back!

A small ceremony, not quite a 'stone laying', was held on the site on 9 May to mark the stage reached and to commit the project to God. It was led by Donald Cranefield and Norman Burke, then Cedarmore Chairman, with Roger Sims, still the local MP, again present. Supportive of the work as ever, Roger had written to the Housing Corporation commending the project to them and doubtless this had played some part in their grant allocation decision. Although there was much work still to be done, this was also an occasion of thanksgiving and indeed rejoicing, not least among Beechmore staff, that 'Ann's project' was at last definitely going forward. There was a feeling that there was more than a human hand behind this project and a quiet confidence that it was going to be used to bring help and blessing to some in special need.

There was a sad aspect of this occasion in that it was the last Cedarmore event of this kind to be attended by Norman Burke. He died suddenly from a heart attack a few months later. Norman was one of the founding members of the Association and had been involved in most aspects of Cedarmore work since its beginning. His wisdom, experience and quiet judgment had been of great value throughout that time and not least when vital decisions had to be made. He was going to be missed.

The building period was not without its problems. At one or two of the site meetings there were clashes with Damien as to exactly what the contractors were expected to provide. But these were settled amicably in the end, not least through the diplomacy of Derek Briscoe and the more reasonable attitude of some of Damien's colleagues.

The builders wasted no time in constructing and finishing the building and actually handed it over to Cedarmore on 9 November 1992. There was work to be done in furnishing and fitting out the building to make it ready for occupation and by Christmas this was very largely completed. After three years of waiting, this was to be a Christmas present and new responsibility for Ann and her staff and the next chapter will show how well they coped with it.

Chapter 19
Florence House

One major decision which had to be made during the construction of the new building was as to what it would be called! As always, there were divergent opinions on this and it took some time for the matter to be resolved. Muriel's house committee could not find a consensus on the issue and decided to ask the staff. Without too much difficulty, they came up with the name 'Florence', remembering perhaps its historical association with good nursing care but more so that it was the sad condition of the resident Florrie or Florence Wakefield which had prompted the desire to develop the special unit. This seemed to strike a chord and that name was readily adopted.

During the long period leading up to the completion of the building, Ann and her senior colleagues gave much thought as to how they were to run the new unit, how it was to be staffed and the extent to which it would be serviced and supervised from the main Home. She wanted it to remain an integral part of Beechmore and be regarded as such by all staff and friends and yet have a separate identity and different kind of care and activity programme. The needs of these residents would be different in many ways from those in the main home. This meant that the staff should have some understanding of dementia and some special training to enable them to cope with meeting their needs.

Fresh staff obviously had to be recruited for this work although there were some existing staff who asked to be transferred to this unit. The attitude of care staff to working with dementia residents was of two kinds. Some felt drawn to it and found real satisfaction from being able to help such dependant and vulnerable people. There were others who found relating to them very difficult and preferred working only with the physically frail. Ann herself, of course, was in the former category and wanted all the new unit staff to share this outlook and was able to demonstrate by example the kind of care and attention that was needed. She also arranged for one or two staff to go on short dementia courses and organised a week's intensive training in the new unit prior to any residents being admitted. A consultant psychiatrist, someone from the Alzheimer's Society and one or two experienced carers in this field voluntarily gave some help in this. Their emphasis throughout seemed to be on treating such residents as normally as possible and on encouraging the use of as many skills as they had left for as long as possible. Hence the importance of activities. Whilst this attitude was accepted and adopted by staff and it seemed very relevant to residents in the fairly early stages of dementia, it seemed less practicable in some cases as the dementia progressed and the resident became wholly dependant on the carer for the smallest of tasks.

But there were high hopes as a full staff team was assembled ready for admission of the first residents in the second week of January. There were also a number of volunteers who had offered to assist at meal times or with activities. During the preceding two months, the house had been furnished and equipped and given as homely an appearance as possible. There was an old-fashioned fireplace with mantelpiece in the lounge and, hanging over it, one of Donald Cranefield's floral paintings which he had presented to the unit. Each of the eight rooms had its en suite toilet and fitted wardrobe. Six of the rooms were on the first floor but a spacious lift allowed easy access to the ground floor and the main lounge and dining area. Main meals were to be cooked in the Beechmore kitchen and brought over. Breakfasts, etc would be prepared and served from the Florence House kitchen. The whole atmosphere was deliberately non-institutional and ambulant residents would even be encouraged to do small tasks in the kitchen if they wished to do so.

During the first week in January, the new unit was visited by Val Hughes, still the Homes Registration Officer for Bromley. She had been consulted on the planning of the unit and, as with the main Home earlier, had given helpful advice and taken a personal interest in it. She found little difficulty, therefore, in recommending registration of the unit as an annex of Beechmore Court to provide this special care and by 11 January 1993 it was ready for admission of its first residents.

News of the project had spread in the local community and within local Church congregations, not least from the Appeal Brochure which had been circulated. It was not surprising therefore that some applications for admission were received from relatives of dementia sufferers with no previous contact with Cedarmore. However, there were four of the existing Beechmore residents and one Southmore resident who were deemed to need this special care and they were amongst the first residents to be admitted. Among them was Florrie herself and Doris to whom we referred earlier. Both took to the change remarkably well and almost from the start were happier and seemed to benefit from the different atmosphere and closer attention which they were receiving. Florrie wandered less and Doris was just happy to be looked after and daily expressed her thankfulness to the good Lord who was providing for her. Two other ladies and one man joined them and within a fortnight this small community of eight elderly people and the small staff was complete. Betty, the other wanderer referred to earlier, had not lived long enough to become one of them. One of the two ladies was Alice, a lovely person who had been cared for by her husband for a number of years but his health and her dementia had now become such that it was impossible for him to do this any longer. She settled well into Florence House and occasionally played the piano which had been provided in the lounge. Visits from relatives were encouraged by the staff and Alice's husband would visit most days and spend several hours with her. He was thus able to continue to share in her care to a degree and give her quality time which had been impossible when acting as her main carer.

The small team of staff which Ann had assembled to run the unit proved to be of a high caliber and shared in the commitment and enthusiasm for making the project a success. The work was demanding, perhaps a little more so than expected. Voluntary help at eating times came to be appreciated. One or two staff discovered, after a month or so, that this was not quite their sphere and left to go elsewhere. Most of the others stayed on for several years and one or two are still working there to-day. One of these is now the senior carer. Continuity of staff with minimum changes was considered important for the residents and enhanced their feeling of security. It also meant that staff got to know well the individual residents and their particular quirks and sometimes some of their past lives, of which they could be reminded.

So, the house being fully furnished its amenities in use, and the family of staff and residents complete, it was time for a little celebration. An Official Opening had been planned for 19 May and Mrs Eileen Cary, wife of Dr George Cary, then Archbishop of Canterbury, had agreed to perform the opening ceremony. This was a great honour for the Association and the Home and the event was a great success. Mrs Cary's own mother had suffered from dementia towards the end of her life and she showed great understanding of the need and the project. The Beechmore lounge was packed for the short service of thanksgiving and dedication led by Mike Nichols and Denis Ellison-Nash, the new Cedarmore Chairman. Representatives of the Housing Corporation, the Tudor Trust and many local churches as well as relatives of the new residents were present. It was a warm Spring day. Refreshments were enjoyed in the garden with a background of piano and flute music played by Iris Emmins and Lizzie Kemp. The whole atmosphere was one of celebration and thanksgiving that this long planned special care project had at last reached fruition and a small number of needy people were already benefiting from it.

Getting the finances of the new unit right was not quite as easy as it may have been thought. The capital funding which might have been a great problem had come relatively easily. In this Cedarmore was again specially blessed. The Florence House Appeal launched by Andrew and Elizabeth received a good response and the remaining £100,000 was gradually raised. Funding the running costs gave initial problems as the budget had slightly underestimated the number of staff hours which would be required to run the unit successfully. There was, of course, a price to be paid for caring within a small family setting. It was soon discovered that the fees originally quoted did not fully cover running costs. A meeting with some of the relatives of residents was called and the position discussed with them. No one wanted staff hours to be cut and most readily agreed to a fee increase. This was not quite so easily obtained in the case of residents funded through DSS and some allowances had to be made. When the new basis for funding the fees of such residents through the Local Authority came into force later, it was possible to negotiate a special fee for this kind of resident. Funding this kind of care was never going to be easy and this has proved to be so. Even so, few, seeing the benefit that this kind of care was bringing to these needy residents and the comfort that it was giving to their loved ones, would doubt that it was more than value for the money required.

A few small changes were made to the Florence House building a few years later and, of course, new residents have come and most have ended their lives there. For most it has been a blessing to them at this last stage of their lives even though their condition has been far from what they or anyone else would have desired. Many tributes to the quality of the care and attention given have been received from relatives of those concerned. There have been difficulties over one or two residents for whom the unit proved not quite suitable but these have been few and far between. The main difficulty perhaps has been coping with the situation when the dementia reaches a severe stage and when this is combined with increasing physical frailty. This naturally leads us on to the next chapter.

Chapter 20
And Isabel

It is often said that success can bring its own problems. This seemed to be true of the Florence House project. Within a few months from its opening it was receiving praise from various quarters and Social Services and some local GP's were commending it. It soon came to be seen as a good example of special care for elderly people suffering from dementia. A national publication on the subject included Florence House as a successful model of a small care unit in a residential setting. A London Hospital consultant, the son-in-law of one of the residents, actually invited Ann to speak to a group of doctors about the project at a seminar for which he was responsible. And, of course, families in the area with a relative suffering from dementia were anxious to hear about this new provision.

As mentioned earlier, when the special unit was first being considered, there appeared to be little care home provision specifically for elderly people with dementia in the area. By the turn of the century, however, several new nursing homes for this kind of resident had been opened. Although this obviously reflected the growing incidence and awareness of dementia at the time, it is not unreasonable to assume that the example of Florence House gave some impetus to this.

Not surprisingly, one effect of the unsought publicity was that Beechmore received many enquiries from families with an elderly relative suffering from dementia and new applications to go on the waiting list. It was obvious that Florence House could help only a fraction of these. There were also one or two other Cedarmore residents who were developing dementia and who were likely to need that special care It was natural, therefore, that some began to wonder whether there was any chance of increasing the number of dementia beds.

At the same time, whilst the pressure for dementia care places was increasing, the demand for residential places for physically frail elderly people seemed to be slowing down. One specific reason for this was the new Community Care legislation which had come into effect in 1993. This effected Beechmore in two particular ways.

Firstly, it encouraged the development of ways to provide care for elderly people in their own homes rather than in care homes. This 'Stay Put' emphasis had become a popular view at the time and had been encouraged by the recent Griffiths Report. It is probably still accepted as generally desirable, whenever practicable. It was thought also to be the wish of most older people - which is probably still true, although not universally so. Where acute loneliness is a problem, as is often the case when there has been a close bereavement late in life, it is surprising how much difference the more communal life of a residential care home can make. Beechmore has evidenced a number of examples of this. The new emphasis doubtless also reflected understandable concern over the growing cost to the community of residential care as people lived longer. 'Care in the Community' has proved not to be cheap although, on the face of it, considerably less expensive than full residential or nursing care.

Secondly, it transferred responsibility for the funding of care for elderly people of limited income from Central Government DSS, to the Local Authorities - whether that care is residential, nursing or domiciliary. Where such funding was needed - in practice for people with savings less than a certain figure (then around £16,000) - the Local Authority would provide this if their Social Services officers concluded that such care was needed. Where they considered that that person's present need could be met through a home care package, the Authority would not fund residential care. Obviously there would be special circumstances and borderline cases and attitudes which differed from one Authority to another - and from one Care Manager to another. But this policy did have the effect of keeping some potential residents in sheltered or private accommodation who might previously have wished to move into a home such as Beechmore.

Like most legislative changes, it took time for the practical effect to be seen but it was soon clear that some of the people waiting for a place at Beechmore who could not be self-funding were likely to be offered personal care at home instead. It was also suspected that, by the time Social Services deemed that care to be inadequate, the need would really be for nursing rather than residential care. It began to look as though the demand for residential care places from physically frail elderly people would be diminishing. Indeed at one meeting of the Beechmore House Committee in December 1995 it was reported that there was only one serious applicant for any vacancy other than for Florence House. Needless to say, that position soon changed and there has never been any serious problem over filling vacancies in the main unit. However, at the time, it did contrast with the high demand for places in Florence House, where any vacancy could be filled several times over. This was partly due to the understandable perception that home care was not quite so appropriate for dementia sufferers, particularly where they were living alone.

There was another aspect of the Florence House situation which was playing on Ann's mind. Even amongst the eight residents there, the severity of dementia varied considerably from one to another and affected them in different ways. Sadly, by its nature the condition tends to deteriorate. Some had already lost all personal skills and had become dependant upon the carers for most basic needs, including dressing, feeding and toileting. In others where the dementia was still mild, it manifested itself mainly in memory loss, and they were still able to do many things for themselves and would respond to mental stimulation and activity which could play a part in delaying the dementia progress. As the proportion in the former category increased demands on the staff increased and allowed less time for attention to the activity needs of the others.

Some would have responded to this situation by suggesting that wholly dependant residents be transferred to a nursing home specialising in elderly mentally infirm (EMI) care. Ann and her Florence House staff did not think that way. She believed that continuity of care in the same environment was important even for severe dementia patients and that, if at all possible, they should be cared for at Florence House until the end of their lives. Staff too became attached to residents and wanted to see them through in this way, notwithstanding the demands upon them.

In this situation it was perhaps not surprising that thoughts began to turn to a) the possibility of increasing the number of dementia places and b) using those additional places for milder dementia cases only. Rather than further expansion which was not really practicable, the idea of turning 8 of the 28 Beechmore general elderly care places into dementia care places began to emerge. Could this be done in such a way as to make those eight new dementia beds into a separate unit something like Florence House? This was the big question.

It so happened that this thinking occurred at the same time as changes were having to be made to the laundry provision in the Home. The small laundry incorporated into the original Beechmore was already proving inadequate for the needs of the Home, particularly with the heavy demands from Florence House. Additional equipment was needed and the room could not contain these. There was still some land space at the back of the main building near to the Florence House link way. Reg Shore and Eric Mountford had come up with a plan for constructing a new laundry room in that space which could accommodate all the laundry equipment needed. Their plan was enthusiastically adopted by staff and house committee and seemed likely to proceed.

This would release some space on the ground floor, close to the nine residents' rooms on that side of the building. Muriel's house committee then began to consider whether this could be the focus for a second dementia unit. It should not be difficult to use eight of those rooms for this purpose but a dining and sitting area was also needed. They turned to Reg to see whether this could be provided in the space available - and again he did not fail them. By changing the use of one or two other small rooms, Reg was able to produce a clever plan which appeared to give what was needed and conform with space requirements. It even included direct access from the dining area on to a small patio which later proved a real asset in warm weather. Although, because of its position, this unit was unlikely ever to be as self-contained as Florence House, it appeared to meet the need and be appropriate for milder dementia care. The plan was discussed with Social Services who approved both the intended increase in dementia provision and the proposed changes. As the project involved some alterations to the building which he had designed, Derek Bingham was invited back from retirement to approve the plans and see through the building changes. Derek was happy to serve Cedarmore again in this way and, although he changed Reg's plan very little, he was able to ensure that a delicate building operation was carried through safely and to a high standard

There was, of course, the question of funding. Here again, Beechmore's needs were to be met in an unexpected way. A member of Orpington Baptist Church, Mrs Isabel Sidey had in her Will bequeathed a sum of money to Trustees to be used for a Christian residential care home for elderly people. After considering how best to use the money for that purpose and exploring the various options open to them and taking legal advice, they decided that it could best be used to assist and develop the work at Beechmore Court. This came at just the time when funds were required for the new laundry, for some improvements which had been found necessary at Florence House and for the building alterations and equipment which were necessary for this second dementia unit. That donation provided all the funds that were needed.

Not surprisingly, when the new unit was opened in October 1996, it was named **'Isabel'** after the lady whose thoughtfulness and generosity had funded it. One of the trustees concerned had been Harold Brooker, who is referred to earlier, and he and his wife Dorothy had been strong supporters of the Beechmore project. A name was now required for that section of Beechmore Court excluding Isabel and Florence House and it seemed appropriate to call this the Brooker section. Those twenty rooms and the main lounge have been known in that way ever since.

Staffing of the new unit was, of course, important. A short time before this opening, a qualified nurse who had worked for a while at the Alzheimer's Day Care Centre in Bromley Common had joined the part-time Beechmore staff. Ann decided to give her the task of supervising the care in Isabel which, of course, she did very well. That lady was Julia Isaacson who a few years later became Head of Home and a great blessing to the whole of Beechmore.

The first Isabel residents settled in well and seemed to appreciate the cosiness of the new lounge area with its outlook on to the garden and its comfortable dining space. Although no attempt was made to prevent those residents from entering the main Brooker lounge if they wished to do so, most soon preferred to be in the small Isabel lounge which perhaps gave them a greater sense of security and closer contact with their carers. As already discovered, perhaps for this reason, dementia residents tend to spend most of their time in the communal area rather than in their own rooms. With other residents the opposite is often true.

So, with Florence and Isabel in full use, Beechmore Court was now a residential care home for 36 people, 16 of whom would have been diagnosed as suffering from some degree of dementia. Although Isabel residents would always be those whose dementia was less severe and more easily managed, it was unlikely, of course, that at any one time the 16 dementia residents would include precisely 8 who could be described as having mild dementia and 8 whose dementia would be regarded as severe! There would always be marginal cases and individual situations where the judgment of the supervisors and Head of Home would be decisive. Nevertheless, the different needs of Isabel residents were soon apparent and staff have endeavored to respond to those needs accordingly.

At the same time, Florence House staff continued to provide that complete care for some of its residents who had become wholly dependant upon them. If anything, the proportion of Florence House residents in that condition has increased over the years and very few of them have been transferred elsewhere. One resident who could certainly be described as dependant in this way is Mabel and telling her story may demonstrate what Florence House has been able to do for this kind of resident.

Mabel, now ninety, is a lady who has spent most of her adult life in the service of others. As a State Registered Nurse, she worked in a London hospital during the Second World War and for a while afterwards. In the 1950's she joined the staff of a nursing home for disabled younger people where she worked for 30 years becoming Deputy Matron and later Matron of that Home. Whenever duties permitted she attended Bromley Baptist Church. She never married and on retirement she began to care for a close friend whose health had failed, eventually committing herself almost wholly to this task. For several years she visited her friend daily, nursing her personally and never taking a holiday. When the friend died, there was a reaction and her own health started to deteriorate. She moved into Southmore Court so as to benefit from the sheltered environment but before very long her memory began to fail and it was obvious that she was developing dementia. She was recommended for residential care and a place was found for her in the Isabel unit. She had a likeable personality and a ready smile and a great 'nurses' sense of humour but her dementia deteriorated and she was later transferred to Florence House where she has now been a resident for eight years. Although for much of that time she retained her cheerful personality, her health continued to deteriorate. She now no longer recognises visitors and is wholly dependant on staff for all her needs.

Mabel's story is typical of several who have lived at the Florence House over the last 15 years and who have been cared for there until the end of their lives. It is to the great credit of Ann, and to Margaret and Julia who have followed her, and to Florence House staff like Gina, who has been there since it opened in 1993, and others that they have not sought to have such residents moved on to establishments providing more intensive care but rather have wanted to give such tender loving care to them for as long as it is needed. In doing this, they have exercised that Christian caring ministry for which the Beechmore project was intended - and carried that commitment far beyond what was ever thought possible. When Cedarmore began its very modest start more than twenty years earlier in providing care and accommodation for a few elderly people through a sheltered housing scheme, no one dreamed that it would eventually, through people like these, be able to minister to such needs as those of Mabel and others like her. Who would not describe their work as vital Christian service - carried out on behalf of the local community and on behalf of the local Churches who are behind Cedarmore? The words of Jesus on 'inasmuch' come readily to mind.

PART V
EXPANDING THE SHELTER

Chapter 21
Elenmore

I guess most observers would agree that, from an aesthetic point of view, Elenmore Court is the most attractive of the Cedarmore properties. The bay windows, rotund stair enclosures, fresh brickwork, small canopy entrance, spacious corridors, even the large paved car park, and now the recently added small conservatory, make it stand out as somewhat exceptional for a housing association development. Usually in such developments cost controls rule out anything in the nature of frills and the emphasis has to be on functional amenities. Yet Elenmore does not appear to be lacking in these. We may reach our own conclusions, as the story unfolds, as to why Elenmore has this quality. There are perhaps several reasons which we shall refer to later.

Another feature of Elenmore Court which distinguishes it from other Cedarmore developments is that it did not come about as a response to a perceived need and after a search to find a site to develop in order to meet that need. Rather it was an opportunity to expand the Association's sheltered accommodation in a different way which arose unexpectedly - and which it did not hesitate to grasp. It came soon after the Florence House project had been completed and when the management committee had plenty of matters to attend to. It was quite a bold decision to take up this opportunity and one which was vindicated later in the successful completion of another project. This project, though different from the others, has also proved a blessing to another small group of elderly people - if the words of some of its residents are to be believed! The circumstances which gave rise to this opportunity are interesting.

The slump in the property market in 1990 which led to the Lime Close site becoming available for the Florence House development continued right through to 1993 and it was well into 1994 before the developers who owned that site felt confident enough to build some of the private houses for which the site was intended. In the meantime, Mission Care who owned the neighbouring Homefield nursing home property, by then around 100 years old, had taken the opportunity to do a deal with the developers for the building of a new nursing home on the two adjacent plots. We hoped that they had found the negotiations easier than Cedarmore had - perhaps Cedarmore had blazed the trail! However, the developers were clearly not confident enough of the market to want to acquire the old Homefield site for housing development and Mission Care needed to dispose of this to help fund the new building. Here again the good relations which have always existed between Mission Care and Cedarmore proved valuable. Both organisations had a vested interest in the right kind of development on this important corner site which adjoined both Beechmore Court and the new Homefield. The logical solution, therefore, was for the site to be developed by Cedarmore in a way acceptable to both parties. This solution seemed to be accepted, in principle, by both parties without any dissent - almost as a natural progression of the garden site purchase for the Beechmore development which had been agreed nearly ten years earlier.

There were, however, several hurdles to be overcome. The first was to agree the nature of any development. Secondly, of course, there was the major one of Cedarmore obtaining funding for both the site acquisition and its development. The third was the problem of agreeing a site value acceptable to both organisations, both of which had to be guided by surveyor's valuations. Finally, of course, planning consent for any development would be required and the Planning Authority were known not to favour, for various reasons, a too intensive development of this corner site. How these hurdles were overcome is perhaps another example of how the work of Cedarmore seems to have been particularly favoured.

A decision as to the nature of the development was reached fairly easily. Certainly this had to be a project to benefit elderly people but, although both Cedarmore and Mission Care were providers of some form of residential care, neither at that time felt that another residential care development or a major extension of Beechmore Court would be appropriate for this site. Beechmore had just opened Florence House and was coping with that special extension of its work. The situation pointed to extending or filling any gap in Cedarmore's sheltered provision and at the same time making use of the close proximity of Beechmore. Fairly obvious gaps in Cedarmore's two sheltered schemes were a) accommodation for couples and b) accommodation for those with a physical disability. It was also unlikely that any permitted development would be large enough to support a resident warden.

The natural answer, therefore, was to develop a small scheme to provide accommodation adequate and suitable for elderly couples, one or two of whom might be disabled, where there would be no warden supervision but with emergency support available from neighbouring Beechmore Court. A brief along these lines was submitted to the architects and they soon came up with an attractive plan for a development of the site to provide nine good sized flats, at least two of which would have special amenities for a disabled person. This was discussed with Mission Care and generally approved and formed the basis of a planning application to the Local Authority. Not unexpectedly, the Planners reduced the site of the scheme to eight flats and made one or two small amendments but eventually issued planning consent in January 1994.

The funding arrangements took a little longer but seemed to fall in place just at the right time. A 'Bid' for a funding allocation for the scheme was submitted to the Housing Corporation at around the same time as the planning application and there was a suggestion that it might be considered for some funding in the next financial year. As it so happened, around the same time the Association received a monitoring review from the Corporation's regulatory department and a visit from the Regional Manager to see Beechmore and Florence House. This was an obvious opportunity to show her the Homefield site and its potential. How impressed she was we never knew but a few months later, after a detailed application had been submitted, Cedarmore were informed that the sum of £363,000 had been provisionally allocated for the project. This was a great encouragement and really sooner than expected. This was later confirmed as a Grant and represented just over 60% of the total cost of the project. Gone were the days when Housing Corporation funding, by combined grant and loan, would cover 95% of the cost of a scheme! Associations were now expected to arrange their own private sector borrowing. By this time Cedarmore had a good standing with National Westminster Bank who seemed happy to provide a long term loan to cover most of the remaining funding required - a loan which had to be serviced subsequently out of the rental income from the flats. A little charitable funding filled the small gap but without the substantial Housing Corporation Grant for the scheme, of course, it could not have proceeded. The visit from the Regional Manager and another letter of support from our friendly Member of Parliament may well have helped in this and once again the timing seems to have been right.

The site valuation, based on the planning consent granted, was left in the hands of the surveyors and they seemed to have no great difficulty in reaching agreement on an appropriate figure. By mid 1994 the nursing home had moved into its new building and demolition of the old building could proceed. Once this was completed, the site acquisition could proceed and on 17 October 1994 Cedarmore found itself the owner of another building site.

Detailed planning of the development could now proceed. We mentioned earlier the special qualities of the building eventually produced. Most of the credit for this must go, of course, to the architect. Derek Briscoe of Fountain Flanagan Briscoe Associates had been a helpful consultant architect for Cedarmore in the Florence House development. With the other Derek now retired, it was decided to ask Fountain Flanagan to be architects for this new development and their partner Derek took responsibility for it. Derek was one of those architects who had a flair for interesting design and the location of this site and the Planning Authority's attitude to its development seemed to call for an application of that skill. The result was a simple but imaginative scheme which still looks special twelve years later.

Cedarmore's own control of the development, too, was particularly strong. By now, it had had no little experience! The management committee had placed full responsibility for all aspects of this development in the hands of four of its most experienced members - Reg, Eric, Ron and Alfred, all now in retirement. They had become used to working together and proved a strong team, meeting regularly once a month throughout the development period. They complemented each other in their differing skills and experience and, as their minutes show, their scrutiny covered all details of the scheme. They developed a good relationship with the Architect and Cedarmore was perhaps uniquely favoured in having such men giving their time to this work.

As building work started, the team was further strengthened when joined by Frank Holt who took on the role of Clerk of Works for the project. His arrival was very timely. Reg Garthwaite who had been such a tremendous help in the building and early days of Beechmore was now quite unwell and sadly died in St Christopher's a few months later. Frank (known to many as Sylvia's husband!) was a retired civil engineer whose more recent professional experience had been in quality control. No one perhaps could have been more temperamentally suited for both quality control and clerk of works roles than Frank! He was able to combine extreme thoroughness in scrutiny of the actual building operation, with friendly relations with the builders, architect and the four man committee. Few could manage that! Frank very quickly imbibed the spirit of the development and its objectives became important to him. He subsequently took a great interest in the welfare of the first occupants and joined the house committee. It was he who first suggested the conservatory which was added several years later although, sadly, he did not live long enough to see it.

The building contract went out to tender in March 1995 and, not surprisingly, when these were received the lowest, from Baxall Construction Ltd, was above the acceptable cost figure. Some pruning had again to be necessary but under the Quantity Surveyor's guidance it was possible to get the figure down to a little over £400,000 which proved acceptable to all parties. The building contract was duly awarded to Baxall and work on site started in fine weather on 12 June. Just a few people attended a brief stone laying ceremony on 18 August, when Mike Nichols committed this further project to God for His protection and blessing.

Building work proceeded reasonably smoothly after some initial problems over infill of the basement of the old Homefield building much of which had been left behind after the demolition. These were resolved satisfactorily but did allow a small part of the old foundations to be left behind in one section of the garden area. The landscape gardeners were not very pleased to discover this when they came along after the building completion. The restriction on plant growth in that particular section of the garden has caused some disappointment and occasional irritation ever since! Perhaps another example of a short sighted cost saving decision, which, in retrospect, may seem to have been unwise. As usual there were a few other problems to be resolved as the building work proceeded. All the team were conscious of the need for cost control in order to keep the final building cost within the finance available. Concern was raised when two of the subcontractors' proposed charges for specific work significantly exceeded the 'PC sums' which the Quantity Surveyor had inserted in the Bill of Quantities for that work. Nothing too unusual perhaps, but it necessitated some urgent further negotiation and trimming to resolve the problem. Much of the detail of the mechanical and electrical services to the building - heating, lighting, lift, fire and emergency alarms, etc, including the link to Beechmore - had to be settled during this period. Here the knowledge and experience of Eric and Reg, proved invaluable as they were able to discuss the details with the architect and specialist subcontractors to ensure they met the requirements of the project. Although at one time the builders appeared to be well behind programme, they seemed to make up much of their lost time and, in the end, handed over the new building in April 1996, only a few weeks behind schedule.

The building as completed was a two storey building containing eight self-contained flats each leading on to a wide corridor which overlooked the garden. Six of the flats had two bedrooms. The other two had one large double bedroom. Two of the ground floor two bedroom flats had kitchen and bathroom amenities appropriate for a disabled person. A passenger lift to the first floor was provided. All flats were designed to take two people and were spacious by earlier sheltered scheme standards. Alarm cords in each flat provided a link to Beechmore Court for emergencies. No communal lounge was included and, in the early years, the pleasant and spacious corridors became the main area for communication between residents. At one stage during the development period, the idea of a communal laundry in place of one of the second bedrooms was proposed but this was dropped and instead each flat was provided with its own washer dryer. This was a decision in favour of individuality although in retrospect it seems that some residents would have preferred communality! Outside, the landscape gardeners designed pleasant garden areas and the attractively paved parking area provided more than enough space for each resident to have a car. In practice only a few ever have - an over provision which has proved very useful to visitors and to some of Beechmore staff!

Unsurprisingly, it was not difficult to find elderly people keen to occupy these new flats and to allocate them to folk who would benefit from living in this kind of accommodation and its proximity to Beechmore Court. Under the financing terms, half of the places had to be offered to the Local Authority and their Housing Department duly suggested allocations for these. This left only four flats for offering to people who had approached Cedarmore direct and soon all the flats were occupied and a small community was coming into being.

By this time, of course, a name for the development had been agreed. Management Committee had wanted it to be called 'Eleanor Court' after the wife of one of the development team. She was not keen on this but suggested a compromise linking that name with the syllable 'more' - which linked it with other Cedarmore projects - hence the name 'Elenmore Court'.

So this scheme was now ready for an 'official opening' and this took place on a windy Friday afternoon on 24 May 1996. Once again Roger Sims (not yet Sir Roger), the local MP, showed his support for Cedarmore work by performing the opening ceremony and Mike Nichols, by then Chaplain of Beechmore Court as well as Bromley Baptist Church minister, led a prayer for blessing on the project and its residents. Around fifty people attended this, including the Bank's representative, and most were duly impressed by the quality and attractiveness of this latest Cedarmore development. More important, all the residents seemed pleased with their new environment and glad to be part of this small new community.

So, another Cedarmore development had been completed and was bringing something new and, hopefully, very beneficial into the lives of fifteen people. There were, of course, management matters to be arranged and procedures to be established - a little more carefully in the absence of a warden. Eric, with his usual efficiency, quickly produced a resident's manual. There were, as always, a few teething problems over the building - such as draught from under the patio doors - fortunately dealt with well before the first winter! But what kind of security and shelter did it give to its residents and how successful a scheme did it eventually turn out to be?

Perhaps the first people to whom to address this question should be some of the residents themselves. There are four residents who moved in at the beginning and were still living there, twelve years later. I know that they would not mind being referred to. One of the first couples to move in was Ron and Iris. Ron died several years ago but Iris, now 90, is still there. They had been living in a small Victorian terraced house in Bromley for several years which was proving unsuitable for them in their advancing years. They loved Beechmore Court as Ron's sister had spent her last few years there and Iris often played the piano for its Sunday services and on other occasions. Both Ron and Iris would say what a difference it made to their lives to move into Elenmore Court. When she lost Ron, the closeness of some of the other residents with whom she had become friendly, became a great blessing to Iris. In more recent years, as her own health has deteriorated, she has found the proximity of Beechmore such a help to her - enabling her to continue to stay in her familiar surroundings for as long as possible.

Another married couple who moved in at the same time was Stan and Louise, who came from what, for them, had been unsatisfactory accommodation elsewhere in Bromley. Both were pleased to be part of this new community and, from the start, decided to contribute to it as well as benefit from it. Stan, a man with many diverse skills, was keen on plants and took a great interest in the garden. At one time, he and another resident took full responsibility for maintaining them although after a time the physical demands of this proved too much for them. A small greenhouse was installed in one corner of the garden and, for many years, Stan grew plants from seeds there. At other times, as well as painting, he has been able to pursue his hobby of baking scones - not a few of which have gone to other residents! Elenmore Court has been a help to them both and, with Louise' health now deteriorating, the Cedarmore concern and the proximity of Beechmore is a comfort to them.

And then there is Maggie, who moved in with her sister, at the time of the opening and quickly settled into her new environment. Sadly her sister died a few years later and since then she, like Iris, has found the friendly community around her a source of support and comfort.

An obvious question would be as to whether the scheme has worked as 'sheltered accommodation' without the presence of a resident warden Has the link with Beechmore been an adequate substitute? The answer to this question must be No - in the sense that it could not possibly give, or was intended to give, what a resident warden (or scheme manager) provides in any normal sheltered scheme. Nevertheless, it has given to residents that sense of security and belonging which would not be otherwise available. Residents know that, if they need help or attention in an emergency, through their alarm cord or pendant they could make immediate contact with a carer at Beechmore and something would be done about it - not dissimilar to the community alarm provision in many sheltered schemes. This Beechmore support has also been supplemented in two ways.

Firstly, at the start, a house committee was established comprising at least one management committee member, the Cedarmore services manager, a Beechmore staff representative, a volunteer interested in the work and one resident, 'the responsible tenant'. This committee has met regularly and has taken an interest in all aspects of the scheme, including the welfare of its residents. The Chairman of that committee, who for many years was Brian Cooper, would visit the scheme regularly and keep in touch with the situation. Periodically, he would arrange for a meeting with all residents and listen to any comments which they had to make.

Secondly, it was initially decided to invite one of the residents to act as the 'responsible tenant' and be a kind of link between residents and management. He or she could report any problems and monitor that they were attended to. This system worked for a while, particularly when, consecutively, two retired nurses were able to exercise the role. When they were no longer available, however, it was not possible to find a replacement and the situation had to be reviewed. After a time, it was decided to recruit a daily 'visitor' who would visit the scheme every week day and make daily contact with each resident whenever possible - as happens in most sheltered scheme. This normally required attendance for no more than one hour per day. As with other Cedarmore schemes, Elenmore was also favoured in this way. When looking for someone to take on this commitment, a retired Beechmore supervisor was found to be willing to do so. It would not have been possible to find anyone more suitable! Barbara gave herself wholeheartedly to this small role, as she would describe it, taking a personal interest in the welfare of each resident and bringing something more to the shelter and friendliness of the scheme. One or two able people who could relieve Barbara when necessary were also found.

Soon after her taking on this role, it was found possible to build a small conservatory leading on to the garden area. This has provided the lacking communal area and Barbara has made good use of it to organise birthday parties and other social occasions. She has even arranged one or two outings.

Most residents, when their health begins to deteriorate, still wish to remain in their sheltered accommodation as long as possible rather than move into residential care. In that situation, the lifeline of support which is available at Elenmore is a great help. It cannot bring in the personal care needed - at present, that is the responsibility of others - but it can take away some of the loneliness and insecurity which physical weakness can bring.

Providing sheltered accommodation for elderly people close to a residential care amenity or within a comprehensive care environment is nothing new although it seems to be practiced more overseas than in this country. Our system does not seem to make a closer or more integrated way of linking the two services very easy. The Beechmore link has helped to make Elenmore the successful scheme and friendly community which it has become. One day, perhaps, someone will see a potential for its giving even more.

Chapter 22
Extending Southmore

In an earlier chapter we referred to Southmore Court as being generally regarded as a very successful 'Category II' sheltered housing scheme and as a friendly and caring community where most residents felt secure and content. It is perhaps not surprising, therefore, that when the possibility of enlarging it a little came along, the opportunity was readily grasped.

The idea of extending it, however, did not come from Cedarmore management but from the neighbouring church, Southborough Lane Baptist Church, which by then had come to see the Southmore Court work as close to its own, with quite a few of its members participating in it. The church had a new building for its regular worship which had been built around the same time as Southmore Court. When their youth work was expanding, the Church felt the need for a new sports and activities hall for this. There was space for this behind the Church building and close to the Southmore Court boundary. The idea occurred to one of their leaders that the building of a new hall could be combined with an extension of the Southmore Court building which would provide several more flats - perhaps with a common boundary wall. The proximity of youth activity to living accommodation for older people did not appear to present a problem! The scheme would involve Cedarmore's buying a little more of the land from the Church but this was not expected to be a problem and would even make a small contribution to the cost of building the hall.

The Church put the idea to Cedarmore and the management committee welcomed it in principle and meetings were held to discuss the proposal and the sketch plans. Those plans suggested an extension comprising eight small flats. There was some reservation over the details and as to whether an extension of this size would be practical and acceptable to the Local Authority. An informal meeting with a Planning Officer was sufficiently positive for them to agree to appoint an architect to consider the proposals and produce some drawings. After some enquiries, it was agreed to ask Derek Briscoe to act on behalf of both the Church and Cedarmore in this. Derek's initial plans reduced the number of flats to six but still linked the two buildings more closely than Cedarmore thought desirable. However, plans to form the basis of a formal planning application were eventually agreed by both parties.

Around the same time, the Southmore warden and residents were finding the communal lounge somewhat inadequate for their many activities, including the regular serving of meals and social occasions. A plan was drawn up for an enlargement of the lounge and this was included in the planning application.

The Council Planning Committee required one or two amendments to the plans and imposed a few conditions but eventually, in April 1990, issued planning consent for the new hall, the additional flats and the lounge extension. The intention was for it all to proceed as one project, as an interesting joint development, with the Quantity Surveyors made responsible for apportioning the building cost.

The main hurdle still to be overcome was the funding - perhaps, nothing unusual! By this time the Church were reasonably confident of being able to find most of the monies for their new hall. Cedarmore was dependant upon Housing Corporation funding for a substantial part of their cost and the project was discussed with a senior Corporation officer at Croydon in 1989. The response was again positive, suggesting the project suitable for 'mixed funding' and recommending a BID for an allocation of funds in the 1990/91 programme. There were pressures on Housing Corporation funds, however, and no allocation for this project was made. Soon after this, too, the Corporation began to rely more upon housing departments of the Local Authority to decide which projects in any particular area should be supported and Bromley saw other housing projects in the area as more urgent than this one. This was understandable although disappointing at the time - and the disappointment continued for several more years. The project was included in the BID applications for several succeeding year without success - until a ray of hope appeared unexpectedly in 1996. The outcome was such that, in retrospect, those disappointments proved to be blessings - because the extension which was eventually built was really more acceptable and of longer term benefit to the Southmore Court scheme than the one which had hitherto been proposed.

Cedarmore management committee was naturally concerned that their inability to proceed with the joint development was preventing the Church from having the new hall which was needed for its youth activities and they encouraged the Church to proceed independently. This called for some revision of their plans but it was probably beneficial and their splendid new hall was built and brought into use in 1995.

During the following year, it appears that the Council found itself unexpectedly with an allocation of funds for sheltered housing and decided to use this in assisting extensions or improvements to existing schemes in the Borough. Associations were invited to apply for a share of this. Cedarmore was invited to bid for an allocation of funds towards both the flats extension project and the kitchen and lounge improvements. It was a great encouragement, therefore, to learn in January 1997 that they had received an allocation of £140,000 towards the cost of both projects which, subject to detailed approval, would be available in the next financial year. The good standing with National Westminster Bank again became useful and, once it was possible to meet their security requirements, a long term loan of £100,000 was agreed. This took care of the balance of funds required. Kay was delighted that at last she would receive her new kitchen and larger lounge - and she was not unduly perturbed that the extension meant that she would soon have several more residents to look after!

In the meantime, there had been second thoughts on the details of the proposed flats extension and its proximity to the Church buildings. Flat space expectations had advanced since Southmore was first built and the provision of six more flats of the same size as the present ones did not seem quite appropriate for the next century. Perhaps a fewer number of larger ones; more like those recently provided at Elenmore, would be more desirable. Derek went back to his drawing board and came up with an attractive scheme to provide just three larger flats, one on each floor, and which, although still necessitating acquisition of additional land from the Church, would allow adequate space and fenced boundaries between the two buildings. All three flats would be large enough to accommodate two people, if necessary. One flat would have two bedrooms and the one on the ground floor would have amenities suitable for a disabled person, as well as open out on to a small patio. There would be access to each flat from the existing corridors as well as an emergency staircase exit at that end of the building.

The revised scheme was discussed in committee and at a meeting with residents and with the Church representatives. With some minor amendments, it was approved enthusiastically. Within the next few months everything seemed to come together quite quickly. Planning Consent and other approvals were granted and working drawings prepared. A site valuation was agreed and the small piece of land transferred from the Church to Cedarmore. The building tender papers went out just a few days before Christmas 1997 and in early February it was possible to accept the Quantity Surveyor's recommendation that W H Simmonds & Son should be awarded the building contract. Work started on site on 9 March 1998 - before the end of the relevant financial year!

Before this, it had been decided to carry out the internal alterations - to provide the larger lounge and new kitchen - completely separately from the new flats project and that work was carried out successfully in the summer of 1997. Needless to say, Kay herself specified much of the equipment for the new kitchen. This seems to have been admired since by most visitors to Southmore Court - and been the envy of other sheltered scheme managers. The ample provision has, however, been well justified since, by the constant use to which this kitchen (and larger lounge) is put for the benefit of residents. Its reputation for facilitating social occasions amongst residents has spread wide and it has demonstrated again that one of the best ways to promote friendships amongst people is for them to eat together!

Cedarmore was again fortunate to have Frank Holt as Clerk of Works on the extension building contract and his presence was particularly valuable in liaison between contractors and architect on one or two of the tricky problems which arise when one building is joined to another - and when people are still living in one of them. It was quite a wet summer and the work fell a little behind programme. Even so, all was completed satisfactorily by October and two of the three flats were occupied before the end of that month. An official opening took place on 13 November, Roger (by then, Sir Roger) Sims once again performing the ceremony, this time taking the form of cutting a tape dividing the old from the new. Donald Cranefield who had led the dedication service for the original building in 1979 was also present to commit this expansion of the work to the One who had manifestly blessed it so far. In his retirement from the ministry, Don had achieved some repute locally for his paintings and, at the special request of Frank, several of these soon found places on Southmore corridor walls

The local authority and the neighbouring church shared in the nomination of residents for the three flats. Two of these were married couples and one a lady with a disability who brought with her, her electric scooter. A small shed where this could be stored and charged was soon provided. Ten years later, that lady by then over 90 was still there, with her scooter. Her enterprise and lively sense of humour had made her a popular resident!

Looking at Southmore Court from the main road to-day, it is difficult to see which part of the building was added in 1998, the external appearance of the extension having so well matched the original. Derek's hand was again evident. The small gap and boundary fence between church and flats is just sufficient to indicate their independence from one another and yet close enough to reveal a mutual interest. Worshippers in the Church may occasionally find themselves distracted by observing movements of elderly people to and from the flats. Residents of the flats, if not themselves sharing in the worship, may catch a sound of the hearty singing from within the Church - or hear the noise of the youngsters playing their band in the Sports Hall. From the rear of the building, residents can watch children arriving for School or playing in the School playground. From the front they can see traffic go by and people waiting at the bus stop. Such is the variety of life - and most residents at Southmore Court are happy not to be completely divorced from it.

This was the last of the expansion projects to be completed. Cedarmore had now to turn its mind to other aspects of its work. They may have been less exciting but perhaps no less demanding on those who were still giving much of their time and energy to its progress.

Chapter 23
Exploring the Boundaries

By now readers may have concluded that, with all its activity in establishing these new projects, there would be little time at Cedarmore meetings for keeping in touch with other developments in elderly care or for exploring new ideas. Certainly there were always full agendas for management committee meetings although much of the detailed consideration of the various items would have been at meetings of the relevant subcommittee. Fortunately, there were always one or two staff or members who made a point of perusing the stream of literature emanating from the various bodies with an interest in housing and care for the elderly. When possible, too, someone would attend meetings of the local federation of housing associations and the local association of registered homes. The exchange of ideas at such meetings could be very helpful and occasionally time would be set aside at management committee meetings to discuss some of the new ideas or developments and their relevance to Cedarmore work. Three of those issues which came up for discussion during the 1990's are worth referring to, not least because they indicate the forward thinking which was still taking place.

The first of these was **Very Sheltered Housing.** This was sometimes referred to as Category 2 ½ Sheltered Housing and perhaps could be roughly described as half-way between warden supervised sheltered housing and residential care. The Care in the Community policy adopted by most Local Authorities from 1993 onwards strongly encouraged residents of sheltered schemes to stay in their flats for as long as possible when personal care was needed, rather than move into residential care. That care would be provided through daily visits from outside carers. Most residents have welcomed this as it avoided, or at least delayed, a move away from the sheltered accommodation and community in which they had settled. Very Sheltered Housing schemes go one step further in providing the personal care, as well as most meals, from within the scheme itself. In theory at least, it gives residents much of what they would expect to receive in residential care whilst still occupying their self-contained flat. The charge for this, although obviously considerably more than the normal combined rent and service charge, should still be well below the cost of full residential care. The care available is unlikely to be adequate for very frail people but could meet many needs.

Some housing associations and private sector organisations have successfully developed schemes of this kind and one would like to think that, if Cedarmore had an opportunity to develop a completely new project, it would be in this form of very sheltered housing where elderly residents could stay for as long as possible. If such a project could combine the friendly and mutually caring community atmosphere of Southmore with the tender loving care available at Beechmore, it would be a very desirable place indeed. A question discussed, of course, was as to whether any of the three sheltered schemes could be converted into such a very sheltered scheme, Southmore being the most likely one. The general conclusion was that the practical difficulties of doing so would not be easy to overcome. There was also a strong feeling that, as Southmore was and still is very successful in its present form, where it already provides more than is available in most sheltered schemes; it would be risky to do anything which might disturb this! This was clearly a wise conclusion although an interesting discussion. It seems that working out the funding of such additional care provision is not easy - although one finds it hard to believe that there is not a way round this, given a little flexibility.

Another issue which arose and was discussed at management committee level was coping with **the incidence of mild dementia amongst sheltered housing residents**. The meeting considered a paper on this subject written by Ann Kemavor who by then had developed a considerable understanding of Alzheimer's and other forms of dementia and its incidence amongst older people. She had been surprised to discover how many folk suffering in this way were able to remain in their own homes at least during its early stages, particularly if there was a caring relative and/or they were able to attend a day centre. She did not advocate that such folk should be admitted into sheltered schemes as they would probably have difficulty in adapting to a fresh environment. However, she did say that when an existing sheltered resident developed the illness, it should not be automatically assumed that they then needed residential care. She felt that, with a little extra support and some understanding from other residents, such a person could stay in their sheltered flat for some time. In that situation, combined perhaps with appropriate medication, progress of the dementia could often be delayed. She was, of course, questioning the 'she should not be here' attitude which had influenced the thinking leading to Florence House several years previously. Management committee members reacted sympathetically to this approach though recognising that each individual case was different and that there could be no hard and fast rules on such a situation. As a general policy, though, it was hoped that Cedarmore sheltered schemes could be like any other caring community, having amongst them one or two mentally as well as physically frailer older people who might need a little more attention and a little more understanding than others. As the condition eventually, almost inevitably, progressed though, Beechmore should now, through Isabel or Florence, be able to give such resident the special care needed.

A third subject which was considered quite seriously around this time, arising from the new **'Care in the Community'** policy was as to whether Cedarmore should become involved in actually providing such care to elderly people who remained in their own homes. In line with Central Government policy, London Borough of Bromley Social Services Department was keen to meet the care needs of as many people as possible in this way. Indeed, their policy became to give financial support for residential or nursing home care only after an individual assessment and a panel decision that it was necessary in that particular case. Bromley were amongst the first Authorities to seek to provide that home care through other agencies rather then through their Social Services department direct - as now seems to be fairly general practice.

Those agencies could be either private businesses or voluntary organisations but, to be used by Social Services, they needed to be accredited in a similar way to care homes. It was suggested at national level that some housing associations which were already involved in providing care and accommodation for the elderly might be appropriate agencies for delivering such home care and could branch out into this kind of service. Several organisations in the Borough were invited to a briefing meeting on the subject at Social Services office - and Cedarmore duly sent its representatives.

They returned with a feeling that this was something which should be seriously considered. In one sense, it was quite different from anything that Cedarmore had been involved in previously, as it had no link to housing or residential accommodation although, of course, it was for the same kind of client. Also, there was at the time a growing thought that the days of residential home care, as distinct from nursing home care, might be coming to an end. If Local Authorities would not financially support residential care for people with limited resources, then Beechmore would not be able to help those people. Those who could be self-funding, too, might opt to stay at home and pay for having care brought to them. In the event, things have not developed quite that way and the demand for places at Beechmore Court has generally continued to exceed the supply. Nevertheless, at the time, this perception will have encouraged some in the Cedarmore team to consider this idea seriously. Others, like the Beechmore Head of Home, simply saw it as a possible new challenge and a different way of ministering to the care needs of older people in the name of a Christian organisation - and indeed as an extension of the work of Beechmore. It was, in fact, one of those 'hot' subjects at the time which even found its way on to the agenda of a Bromley churches forum. Mike Nichols was keen to see churches involved in such work and warmed to the idea of Cedarmore being one of the vehicles through which it could be provided.

Time was spent on working out how such a service could be organised and financed, using Beechmore as its base, and an early retired Crofton Church member had offered to organise and manage such a scheme for us. It was soon obvious that there were several risks involved in going down such a road and some likely pitfalls. Even so, some saw it as yet another opportunity which, in the fullness of time, could develop into an important and relevant part of Cedarmore ministry. A proposal to test the water in a very small way was put to Management Committee and an interesting discussion followed. It was another of those discussions between the enthusiasts and the more level-headed and, in the end, the more level-headed ones won the day! They strongly felt that, with the projects which Cedarmore had in hand around that time - Elenmore, Isabel and Southmore extension - and the management responsibility which was becoming more demanding with the increasing regulation, the Association was not in a position to venture into unknown territory of this kind which could become very time-consuming. It was in great danger of becoming overstretched. And, of course, by any logical standards, they were right.

Yet, in retrospect, it seems disappointing that, neither Cedarmore nor any other church-linked or voluntary organisation in the Borough appears to have felt able to become involved in this very practical form of service for older people, many of whom would be living alone. There are now quite a few private home care agencies in the Borough, some providing a very good service and nationwide the practice has spread enormously, giving varying degrees of satisfaction. It would have been interesting to see such care being provided through a voluntary organisation such as Cedarmore, supported by a residential care home and perhaps loosely linked with the pastoral care of local faith communities. One would have expected this to give that added dimension which would have benefited its recipients. Yet the work involved could have become considerable and Cedarmore was certainly not alone in deciding that this would have been a step too far.

The decision to throw out this idea, too, was perhaps a message to the visionaries within the organisation that the time for expansion and new developments was coming to an end - at least for a while. It was now time to consolidate, to organise the management better, to reflect on what had been achieved and to prepare for the future in a changing environment. And that message was read, accepted and followed, intentionally or otherwise, during the succeeding years. With completion of the Southmore extension in 1998, the Association had, in its four schemes, over 90 residents to whom they had a responsibility. This was no light responsibility for a small voluntarily managed organisation, as the final chapters will show. Ten years later, although there have been many improvements, the number of residents has hardly changed - but the work, though in some ways more difficult, has continued unabated.

Part V1
KEEPING THE SHIP AFLOAT

Chapter 24
Looking after the Fabric

As any home owner knows, buying even a newly built property does not relieve one of potential problems with regard to maintenance of either the building fabric or the fixtures and equipment which he incorporates into it. In any new building, there are likely to be a few teething problems. As time goes on, it will need some repairs and re-decorating and equipment will need to be replaced. If it is let to someone else, the tenant will not be slow to call upon the owner if he finds that the doors will not close properly or that the heating system is faulty. Where the landlord owns several properties and each of them is occupied by 20 or so people and the terms of that occupancy are such that the landlord accepts responsibility for both internal and external repairs, it would be surprising if he did not see property maintenance as a major contractual responsibility.

Where that landlord has provided the accommodation, partly to relieve its elderly residents of anxieties and problems of a kind that they wish to be freed from at their time of life, that responsibility has an added ethical dimension. Moreover, should that landlord ever become slack in attending to necessary maintenance, particularly where it might affect the welfare of any resident, it is fairly certain that the Warden or Scheme Manager at the property concerned would not be slow to bring the matter to her employer's attention. After all, her first responsibility is the welfare of each resident. In the Cedarmore situation, the problem is also likely to receive an airing at the relevant house committee meeting and be referred to in its minutes.

Any good landlord, too, would want to take a long term view of its property preservation and take steps to keep its buildings and fixtures in good condition by regular attention and cyclical maintenance. As a registered housing association or registered social landlord, as it is now called, Cedarmore should be able to demonstrate to its regulatory body, the Housing Corporation that it was following that policy and was including adequate maintenance expenditure in its annual budgets.

Property owners are also, from time to time, likely to see a need or an opportunity for improvements - maybe arising from design weaknesses which have been discovered or new needs of occupants or their changing expectations. Over a period of 30 years, and with the increasing frailty and changing needs of residents, it is not surprising that Cedarmore has found itself frequently considering suggestions for improvement to its buildings and amenities or to its plant and equipment.

So how did Cedarmore with its small team and frequent development activity cope with this major landlord responsibility? In the eyes of most of its residents, I think, and in the view of its regulators, it seems to have done quite well. This chapter endeavours to show how that has been achieved.

As with any project or task, the first and perhaps most important decision is to allocate responsibility. Cedarmore did this in its usual way through a special sub-committee - delegating that responsibility to a few of its members who had the relevant skills and experience - and Cedarmore was again fortunate in having such men able and willing to serve in that way.

Soon after the completion of Southmore Court, this Fabric Committee, as it became known, was set up under the chairmanship of John Fagg, an experienced architect who held a senior position on the staff of Greater London Council. He was joined by Reg Shore whose engineering and management experience has been of tremendous benefit to that committee ever since. When John moved away from the area in 1992, Reg took over chairmanship of this committee and continued to do so even when, a few years later, he also became chairman of the management committee. One or two other joined it and Reg Garthwaite, too, was co-opted on to the committee. His practical building experience and down to earth knowledge of most building matters was invaluable.

When he had to leave the committee due to failing health, his place was taken by Frank Holt, to whom we have referred earlier The group was strengthened further when Ron Dungate joined it. Few small housing associations could have had a stronger or more qualified team to look after their properties!

Even so, in the early nineties it became obvious that there was a need for a part-time Services Manager who would keep in close touch with all maintenance and equipment matters and be responsible for seeing that the decisions of the committee were carried through. Eric Mountford took on this responsibility and carried it very conscientiously for several years before handing it over to Brian Withers. Although he has seen his workload expand year by year, Brian has warmed to the role, seeing it as a great opportunity to help older people and to share in the work of Cedarmore. He has met regularly with Fabric Committee members who have continued to carry the main responsibility. Eric himself became a leading member of that committee (and of the management committee) and a tremendous help on this important side of the work. His technical knowledge and experience and commitment to the work was invaluable.

Managing the property in this way has been time consuming for the people involved, but the fabric committee system seems to have worked well as a means of regularly reviewing and maintaining the fabric of the buildings and the efficiency of their services.

It is unlikely to have worked so well, though, were it not for the lesser known men in each of the schemes who, over the years, have been employed to carry out the day to day maintenance, attend to minor breakdowns, report problems and assist residents. They have sometime been described as the 'handymen' although generally referred to as the maintenance staff. Nearly all these men had reached normal retirement age and were happy to work part time for a few more years - in one or two cases, for nearly ten! Most have been popular with residents and have become valuable members of the caring team in each scheme. Some associations will have peripatetic maintenance men who exercise this role but the practice of employing just one person in each scheme has had many advantages. He can become well known to residents, develop a good relationship with the Scheme Manager and find himself relating well to the ethos and objectives of the project So it seems to have worked out.

Perusing the minutes of this Committee over the last 25 years, it is fascinating to observe the diversity of matters discussed and problems dealt with. As well as the regular internal and external decorating and servicing of plant and equipment, there were boiler breakdowns and heating problems, blocked drains, guttering repairs needed, artex ceiling problems, lift breakdowns, locks not working properly, entry phone difficulties, call system weaknesses, problems with laundry and kitchen equipment and much more. The list of potential problems is almost endless. Some problems appear insoluble. In 1983 there was much concern over the irregularity of the hot water supply in one or two of the flats at Southmore and action was taken to remedy this. The October 2007 minutes refer to problems arising when residents in end flats try to use hot water very early in the morning. Presumably no one expected residents in a sheltered scheme for elderly people to want an early morning shower! In 1994, the Beechmore Head of Home was complaining that some toilet seats were cracking and asked for these to be replaced with stronger ones!

As well as dealing with these diverse repairs and renewals, however, much attention was being given to a wide range of improvements suggested by scheme managers, sometimes through their house committees, or by residents themselves at resident consultation meetings. Generally, the policy would be to try to accept such suggestions if they were practicable and beneficial to residents as a whole and could be funded out of normal income. Where this was not possible, an improvement or new equipment would often be paid for out of the residents' Amenity Funds, raised through Summer and Christmas Fayres and similar activities. Larger improvements have sometimes been met from legacies received - in several cases from past residents. Much of the additional equipment which became necessary at Beechmore Court as residents have become frailer, such as hoists and special beds, has been funded in this way. All such improvements were expected to be approved by the Fabric Committee.

As part of the energy efficiency drive, and hopefully to save regular maintenance costs, most of the timber framed windows in all schemes were replaced by PVC framed double-glazing, funded largely through special Grants for that purpose.

All Cedarmore schemes were constructed to meet building and living space standards relevant at the time - either the Parker Morris standards or those specifically laid down by the Department of the Environment. In the year 2000, however, the Department published its new Decent Homes Standards and housing associations were expected to meet those standards in all their schemes by 2010. Both Cedarmore Court and Southmore Court had been built over 20 years in 2000 and by then few of the kitchens and bathrooms met those new standards. Thanks to some tremendous work on the part of Ron Dungate, a programme for bringing all those kitchens and bathrooms up to the required standards was put together and the work completed by 31 March 2008. This meant, amongst other things, all bathrooms being provided with either showers or walk-in baths - a provision greatly appreciated by many residents who were finding it difficult to get into (and out of!) a traditional bath. Half of the cost of this work was funded by a special Repairs Grant from the Housing Corporation.

Around the turn of the century, housing associations were asked to start building up sinking funds out of rental income to meet the cost of future major repairs and to make a special 'rent uplift' to cover this. Eric carried out a remarkable 'crystal gazing' exercise to work out the amount required for this and that fund had been steadily building up since - enabling it to make a substantial contribution towards the cost of the Decent Homes Standards work.

Thanks to the hard work of those on this fabric committee and others who have worked with them, Cedarmore properties are probably to-day in very good shape and well equipped. The fabric appears to be in healthy condition and the plant and equipment is being well used and regularly serviced. The procedure for ensuring this appears to have worked adequately over the years. But it will be no easy task for the successors to the present capable and committed team to see that this continues.

Chapter 25
Balancing the Books

'Money is the root of all evil' says the old song - misquoting, of course, St Paul's first letter to Timothy where he warns against the <u>love</u> of money. The truth is that, however much we may wish to keep money out of the discussion and concentrate on service and compassion and high standards, as we all know it is difficult to get very far in charitable work without it. It is one of the essential tools which has to be available, and which we have to learn to control safely and use wisely.

Certainly, Cedarmore could not have progressed very far in achieving its objectives without the substantial monies which have been invested in it from public funds, banks, charitable trusts and private donations. As we have seen with each of the projects described in this story, funds from those sources became available in quite remarkable ways as they were needed - and those schemes still exist and thrive to-day, providing the care and secure accommodation for their residents. It would be difficult for anyone visiting those schemes and learning a little about them, not to feel that the money invested in them from these various sources has been well spent and is still yielding a good return.

However, although raising such funds was not always straightforward and was not achieved without some anxiety at times, it was in some ways easier and the anxiety shorter-lived than has been the ongoing task of ensuring that the monies coming in from the fees and rents and service charges are sufficient to cover all the running costs and outgoings. True, in the early years of sheltered housing there were revenue deficit grants which could be applied for to cover income shortfalls. This was a system which hardly encouraged efficiency and it is not surprising that such grants were withdrawn after a time. Since then, charitable housing associations, like any business, have had to carefully budget their expenditure and endeavour to ensure that it was kept within the income available from the charges to residents. This has not always been easy - on either the income or the expenditure side.

Controlling expenditure is never popular with either staff or residents - although older people often seem to understand the need for this more than others. Their memories of war time shortages have not entirely left them! But a staff or committee member may well see how their scheme or the welfare of residents, or that of one particular resident, could benefit from some additional expenditure - perhaps by a new piece of equipment or by an additional member of the staff. As the welfare of residents is at the heart of the work, the instinct is to respond positively if the proposal is sound - and this can be difficult if funds are not available. As noted in the previous chapter, one way to fund small improvements has been to invite house committees and resident representatives to do so themselves - through their Amenity Funds. Some very useful improvements have been provided this way but, of course, this has its limitations and cannot apply to regular recurring expenditure.

Controlling staff expenditure has not been easy. As this usually amounts to between 75 and 80% of total expenditure, its importance is obvious. Whilst such control must never prevent their being sufficient staff available to adequately fulfill the association's obligations, there are times, particularly in residential care, when some additional staff or help can make a lot of difference. But it is often difficult to pay for this out of the income available. Sometimes Cedarmore's voluntary supporters have come along and provided such services on a voluntary basis. Escorting residents, organising activities and entertainment, office reception, and even help with the feeding of very frail residents has been regularly provided in this way.

There are restraints on income, as one would expect. Until recent years, those restraints caused few problems on the sheltered housing side. The 'fair rents' agreed with the Rents Officer were usually adequate to cover running costs and ordinary maintenance. Where residents could not afford to pay the fair rent out of their income, they could obtain Housing Benefit to cover the difference. As fair rents have been phased out and assured tenancy rents brought in, the Authorities understandably have taken steps to control these. A somewhat complicated mechanism was introduced but the more simple way has been to place a 'cap' on annual increases, roughly in line with inflation. One can hardly object to this although, as most employers discover, staff and other costs have a habit of increasing more rapidly than the Retail Price Index. Perhaps this is a good discipline and there appear to have been few cases of residents having difficulty in meeting the rent and service charges payable. Quite a few have been grateful to Brian for helping them with their Housing Benefit Claims! The new 'Supporting People' system introduced fairly recently to fund welfare costs in sheltered schemes seems to have brought unnecessary financial complications and one or two financial risks, to no apparent advantage. Hopefully, that system will not have a long life.

Ensuring residential care home income is adequate to cover all outgoings has been a more difficult task and has caused a few headaches from time to time. As the annual outgoings have reached over £750,000, it has clearly not been a task to take lightly. Moreover, as the organisation is a charity whose main objective is to assist and help older people in need, its starting point in agreeing its charges to those residents has always been as to what is the minimum that needs to be charged in order to cover all running costs and other expenses and perhaps set a little aside for future or unforeseen maintenance. It does not, like many businesses, start off with 'what is the maximum that the market will bear'. Even so, sometimes surprisingly, the two formulas can give a similar result! Certainly for many elderly people the idea of paying £400 or more per week 'for their keep' alarms them, even though they may have sold or be able to sell the house which they no longer need for £250,000 or more. They, of course, will have been hoping to pass on part of that sum to their children. Even if most now accept that eating into that capital may well be necessary, the annual fee increases which become necessary do cause them concern and a caring provider will not want to charge more than necessary. Yet the reality is that the residential care fees charged have only been kept at their present levels by keeping a strict watch over expenditure, including particularly the number of staff and the hours worked by them - and by keeping the basic rate of pay at levels which may be in line with the market but are lower than what a caring employer would really wish to pay.

If this kind of consideration has had the effect of restricting fee charges even for self-funding residents, the restraint has been even greater in the case of residents whose fees are met or subsidised by a Local Authority. These often represent about half of the residents - and, of course, they are just as much the people for whose welfare the Home exists as are those who are able to be self-funding. Whilst Local Authorities have generally been willing to cover residential care fees, after they have assessed an elderly person as needing such care, most Authorities have set ceilings on the amount which they will pay. In many cases, such ceiling seems to have been the fee charged by the cheapest home in the Borough! In the early days of Beechmore this ceiling (or the DHSS ceiling before Local Authorities became involved) was very close to the agreed Beechmore charge and the small shortfall could be covered without difficulty. However, the Authorities annual increases in those ceilings have often been below, or no more than, the bare RPI increase, failing to take into account some abnormal or essential cost increases (sometimes imposed on the Home). The result has been that over the years there has developed a not insignificant gap between what Beechmore has considered it necessary to charge and what the Local Authority has been prepared to pay. Such a gap has continued to exist although there may now be a little more flexibility on the part of some Authorities. This, of course, has been the subject of much public discussion and Councils have justified their policy on the grounds of the budgetary restraints imposed on them by Central Government. Those restraints have certainly been real. Nevertheless, this has caused problems for most residential care homes and for those seeking to balance the Beechmore books. It has also led to some robust discussion!

The difficulty can be overcome, or ameliorated, in some cases by 'top-up funding' from relatives or friends of a resident. At one time this was considered illegal but is now permitted and recognised by Local Authorities. It is often built into the individual Agreement with the Council. Often, however, there have been no relatives willing or able to cover the shortfall. Beechmore has built up a Hardship Fund provided from charitable donations specifically for helping in this situation and has drawn upon this in individual cases where no top-up is available. Whether this Fund would be large enough to meet the demands on it, if the proportion of residents' dependant upon Local Authority funding increased substantially is questionable. So far it appears to have been adequate but this is an area where the organisation's ingenuity and faith have been tested over the years.

It would be only fair to record that this situation led to some heart searching and serious debate at one or two committee meetings. There were one or two so concerned over the possible effect of such income shortfall on Cedarmore finances that they seemed prepared to advocate a policy of refusing to accept Local Authority sponsored residents unless the full Beechmore fee was promised. It is questionable whether they were really prepared for such a policy to be implemented in practice or simply wanted to adopt it as a negotiating stance with the Authority. I suspect the latter. Even so, the idea horrified some of those who had been involved in the work of the Association for many years as it seemed to cut right across its original charitable objectives of 'providing amenities for elderly persons upon terms appropriate to their means' and its Mission Statement reference to making its accommodation and care available on terms affordable to those with low income.

Any such change of policy would hardly have gone down well, too, with those bodies and people whose charitable funding had enabled the project to come into being. Fortunately, the idea was not pursued and the doors to all Cedarmore schemes remained open to people in need irrespective of their financial means. The fact that any such restriction was suggested, however, indicates the level of concern which was being felt at the time over this under-funding. One or two did not see why the Local Authority should receive a service for less than its cost. They saw it as a recipe for financial disaster. Most realised, though, that the service was not really for the Local Authority but for the individuals concerned whose needs were paramount and that there had to be other ways of solving that problem.

A major factor affecting adequacy of income to meet outgoings in both sheltered and residential care schemes is, of course, the degree of occupancy. Although it is normal to expect some 'voids' during the course of the year, arising from resident changes, etc and to allow for this in the Budget, gaps in the occupation of one flat or room for any length of time can lead to a significant drop in income whilst running costs remain unchanged. Although there have been a few very short periods when, for specific reasons, one or two rooms or flats have remained unoccupied for several weeks, the demand for places in Cedarmore schemes has generally been such that, when a room or flat has become empty, a new occupant has soon been found. There has been an awareness of the financial effect of under-occupancy so that, during most years, the loss of income through this has been remarkably small - another way in which Cedarmore seems to have been favoured.

So, overall, it was certainly no easy task to balance the books and keep expenditure, including interest payments and overheads, within the income available. In some years it was possible to achieve this and end the year with a small surplus. In other years this was not possible - but over the years surpluses have covered the deficits, if not by a very large margin. Perhaps, for a charitable non-profit making organisation, this is as it should be!

But how did Cedarmore with its largely voluntary administration and small administrative staff manage to control its finances and achieve this reasonably satisfactory outcome? Prior to the opening of Beechmore, the accountant honorary treasurer kept a close eye on all income and outgoings from both projects. When he retired and the Beechmore project was on stream, Management Committee decided to appoint another subcommittee, the finance committee, to look after most financial matters and that committee has remained active in managing the Association's finances ever since.

Comprising two or three accountants and one or two others with a financial or business background, this Committee would meet at least three times a year and make decisions or recommendations on most financial matters. In particular it would agree an annual Budget and consider variations from it during the year. It would recommend the level of rent and service charges for each sheltered scheme and the fees chargeable for Beechmore. It would study the quarterly management accounts and annual statutory accounts produced by the accountant and thus soon become aware of any financial problems which might be developing. Undoubtedly, this Committee can take much of the credit for Cedarmore's finances remaining sound throughout most of the twenty or so years since its formation.

But it needed someone reliable to do the groundwork and provide it with accurate and up to date information. Here again, able people became available. When the running of Beechmore Court was being planned, it became clear that it would need to have at least a part-time accountant on the staff to handle both payroll and other expenditure and collect the fees chargeable etc. As mentioned earlier, the kind and friendly Bert retired just in time to take on this role. His near 'copper plate' writing in the books was a joy to behold and he never made a mistake! When he retired several years later, another retired accountant joined the staff and kept all the accounts of the Association, again preferring to stick to manual records. He, too, was meticulous in his accuracy, loved the work and would provide handwritten schedules for the finance committee almost on demand. When he retired in 2001, another semi-retired qualified accountant joined the part-time staff. He was able to computerise much of the financial records and this greatly facilitated the provision of regular information for the finance committee and the meeting of statutory accounting responsibilities. He, too, seemed to enjoy the work and the responsibility and found himself relating to the objectives of the organisation. Each of these men would keep in touch with the finance committee chairman in between meetings and their work has been vital in enabling the committee to do fulfill its role and keep the finances under control.

So, through these helpful people, this simple financial management structure and its careful control and monitoring of both expenditure and income, notwithstanding a few headaches, the books have balanced reasonably satisfactorily and at 31 March 2008, the finances appeared still to be in good shape. In this, too, Cedarmore has much for which to be thankful.

Chapter 26
Taking Control

We are nearing the end of our story but this would not really be complete without some information as to how Cedarmore as an organisation has been managed over the years and how it has held together as its responsibilities have grown, its staff increased and different people become involved in its work. In to-day's language perhaps we are talking about its 'governance'. In Paul Martin's helpful book 'The Christian Charities Handbook' he says that 'if the charity does not have good governance, then it is likely to suffer, be it from a lack of direction, policy, long term strategy or shared vision'. Few running a charity or business would dissent from this.

Perhaps the form of governance applied in Cedarmore has become fairly obvious as the story has been told. Ultimate responsibility has rested entirely upon the small team of people, normally about ten, who have formed its management committee. That committee has delegated much of its work from time to time to subcommittees, and occasionally to one or two individuals. However, those subcommittees and individuals have always been accountable to the management committee, which has taken full responsibility for the running of the organisation and for all actions taken. As the saying goes 'the buck stops here'.

There are those who would argue that a committee is not the most effective and efficient way of running a business or other organisation, claiming that it can lack decisiveness and prevent speedy action when that is desirable. That, of course, can sometimes be the case. They would claim that vesting final authority in one person can avoid stalemates and facilitate quick decisions when they are needed. This too is true but it carries the risk of precipitous action and rash judgment. Where charitable and public resources are involved, that is a risk which cannot be taken. The management committee members, or Board members as they are often described, are trustees and each has to share in the responsibility.

Where the committee system may need more defending is in relation to delegation of specific tasks or responsibilities to subcommittees. It may seem easier and more efficient just to delegate to individuals and let them be individually accountable to the management committee. However, in that way the organisation loses the benefit of the closer and perhaps broader consideration of a subject which a subcommittee covering that area of responsibility is able to give.

Rightly or wrongly, Cedarmore, over most of its history, has followed the subcommittee pattern and operated largely by delegating specific responsibilities or tasks to small subcommittees. Often individuals have been accountable to those subcommittees. All subcommittees have been expected to contain at least two management committee members and have usually been able to co-opt on to them two or three other people with special interest or expertise in that aspect of the work. Quite remarkably in a way, over the past thirty or more years, it has nearly always been possible to find people happy and willing to share in the work in this way. This is an indication of the local interest in the work and of the Church congregations' support for it and is another way in which the work has been blessed. Generally, the efficiency of operation and the quality of management does not seem to have been impaired by this pattern. On the contrary, there would seem plenty of evidence that the work has been helped and strengthened by the involvement in this way of a larger number of people and by their contributions.

Even so, it has probably only succeeded because three factors have been present most of the time - three factors, which seem essential if such a system is to operate. They are commitment, clarification of responsibilities and coordination. When any of these have been weak, difficulties have been likely to arise. It is worth seeing how those three factors have been present and their effect upon the smooth running of the organisation.

The commitment to the work of most of the people who have served on the various committees has been very evident. Management committee attendance has averaged around 80% at most meetings and most subcommittee attendance has been similar. And, in most cases, those people have been depended upon for considerably more than just attendance at meetings. Most have accepted individual responsibilities for specific tasks or reports or visits and it has been possible to rely upon them. Such self discipline on the part of people who are giving their services voluntarily makes management so much easier. If it is not present and tasks do not get performed, there can be problems. There are no disciplinary procedures, as exist in an employer/employee relationship! Perhaps the main reason for this commitment has been the shared ethos and belief in the value of the work. Folk have seen their contribution as a form of Christian service

Commitment on the part of staff too has been just as vital and this has been present amongst most staff, not only those in senior positions. This again is because most staff seems to have been able to relate to the spirit of the work and share in its objectives. Inevitably, in an organisation like Cedarmore, considerable freedom has to be given to scheme managers and responsibility for day to day operations delegated to them. Their loyalty and commitment to the work has helped to make voluntary management possible. This has not avoided the need for adherence to proper staff policies and procedures and internal control arrangements but only occasionally have they had to be referred to.

Clarification of the specific responsibilities of subcommittees and staff is of paramount importance. In the case of subcommittees, standing or ad hoc, these have been laid down in the terms of reference approved by the management committee for each one, which also define the limits of their authority. As we have seen, steering committees were set up to advance and control each development. These closed once the project was completed and were succeeded by small house committees for each project. As we have also seen, fabric and finance matters have had separate committees. Two small subcommittees have dealt with filling of vacancies - one for sheltered and one for residential care places. Minutes of all subcommittee meetings are taken and copies circulated to management committee members for discussion at their meeting as necessary.

Clarification of the responsibilities of individual members of staff is, of course, essential if any organisation is to run smoothly. This is partly done through job description but sometimes more detailed clarification is required where duties or responsibilities overlap. Where these are not clear, tasks can be neglected or confusion arises. There was an unfortunate case of this when a new senior post was created at Beechmore Court. The decision to make the appointment was sensible enough but the precise relationship between the holder of the new post and the person whose responsibilities were being changed was never clearly defined. Each interpreted their roles differently. The problem was resolved eventually but not without some unpleasantness. The lesson was well learned that job descriptions needed to be clear on both responsibilities and accountability, both at the time of appointment and at any subsequent changes.

But even when responsibilities are clear and the people involved are very committed, this kind of management can run into difficulties unless there is adequate coordination between the various committees and between them and senior staff. In more recent years in Cedarmore there has been one person appointed as Coordinator with the specific task of seeing that the management system was working, responsibilities allocated and information disseminated. This has worked well. Prior to this much of the coordination was left to the Secretary who would ensure that minutes of all subcommittee meetings were seen by the management committee and important matters brought on to its agenda. Each subcommittee chairman would have a slot on those agendas and he would be expected to report on his sector at the meeting. In this way the management committee has been able to keep track on everything of importance happening within the Association, including the general welfare of residents and staff. Regular meeting of that main committee has been an essential element in ensuring coordination of the work. In between meetings or where one has had to be postponed, much reliance has been placed on certain members of that committee keeping in touch with each other and with what is happening.

In Cedarmore, as in most organisations, a vital coordinating role has also been exercised by the chairman of the management committee. Whilst the precise role of the chairman and the closeness of his involvement has varied from one chairman to another, his ability to follow all aspects of the work and to ensure fair discussion and thoughtful decisions at meetings has been vital. Although probably his most important role has been to chair management committee meetings and to give leadership there, he has also been a figure head and representative of the management - both to residents and staff and to the outside world. Over the last forty years six outstanding men have given their time and energies to serve Cedarmore in this way.

All were men who had carried major responsibilities in business or professional life and most too in the life of their local churches - three had been deacons at Bromley Baptist Church. Their leadership experience greatly helped in holding the organisation together as well as enhancing its credibility. Most notable, perhaps, was the contribution of Reg Shore who, as well as chairing the fabric committee and using his engineering and design skills on so many occasions, chaired the management committee for over ten years until retiring from that committee under its 'over 80' policy. Cedarmore became a major part of Reg's life during his retirement from business and a work which he loved to do. He was a 'consensus' chairman, seeking to get an agreed decision from committee members, rather than impose his views on the meeting. This may have made his task difficult at times and perhaps cost him occasional lack of sleep but his knowledge of and involvement in most aspects of the work helped to ensure that it was coordinated - and that it retained the Christian base which was so important to him.

Some time was spent during the mid -1990's in reviewing the structure of the Cedarmore management and considering how best this should operate when several members of the team would no longer be available. Perhaps lacking confidence that there would be people willing and available to serve voluntarily to the same extent as they had themselves, the leaders decided to change the form of management and appoint a director or chief executive to manage the work of the Association on their behalf. A full description of the responsibilities involved was drawn up and, after one or two abortive interviews, a very able and experienced person with a financial background became interested in the position and the committee enthusiastically appointed him Chief

Executive. He shared the ethos of the work and was conversant with modern communication and administrative methods. In these and other ways he was able to bring some of the administration up to date and gave a great deal of time and thought to it - at a time when one or two projects were in their early days and the emphasis was on consolidation rather than development. Unfortunately this coincided with a period of financial difficulties particularly in relation to the residential care scheme and in Local Authorities' funding for this. There was also reluctance on the part of some management committee members to hand over responsibilities to an executive. They had put so much into the work themselves and were perhaps not really willing to trust someone else to do it on their behalf. It seemed that, in some ways, Cedarmore was not quite ready to be run in this way. Perhaps partly for this reason and particularly on account of the financial situation, when the Chief Executive became due for retirement it was decided not to make another similar appointment but to revert to a voluntary committee management system as previously.

The committee structure itself was then reviewed and streamlined so as to place management of all the Association's affairs in the hands of four subcommittees directly accountable to the main management committee. These were the two service committees - finance and fabric - and two operational (or executive) committees - one for the sheltered housing and one for residential care - a fairly logical breakdown of the work. Notwithstanding some misgivings when this revised structure was adopted, it appears to have worked remarkably satisfactorily for the past six years - due in no small way to the strength and commitment of those responsible for chairing these four committees. The big question, of course, is as to whether when these capable men have to retire from this work to which they have given so much of their time, there will be successors found able and willing to serve likewise. That question perhaps can be left until our final chapter

The great thing would seem to be that it has been possible to demonstrate again that a small local organisation like Cedarmore can be managed largely on a voluntary basis where there is sufficient commitment on the part of the people involved and a clear understanding on responsibilities and if there is efficient co-ordination of activities. To these perhaps should be added a shared ethos and belief in the value of the work. This is much more likely to exist, of course, if those involved in the leadership share the same faith and have similar Church allegiances. In such a situation, the fellowship arising from working together in a work of this kind can be very precious and rewarding in itself.

The question may well be asked as to how Cedarmore has managed to remain an independent local organisation for nearly forty years when so many organisations of its kind have sooner or later merged with other small organisations or been taken over by larger ones. Certainly the Housing Corporation has from time to time specifically encouraged both of these and there have been approaches from other bodies to this end. Around the time that Southmore Court was developing, there was a discussion with the Baptist Housing Association who were then developing similar schemes all over the country with the participation of local churches. There was clearly a case for joining with them but the decision was made to remain independent for as long as possible. As BHA itself later merged with a larger housing association, there is now some satisfaction that that option was not pursued. It is also doubtful whether even BHA a few years later would have wanted to take the risk of becoming involved in a residential care project like Beechmore.

The general view seemed to be that, whilst local people were available and willing to take the management responsibility, the Association could best do its work and fulfill its objectives as an independent local organisation. The regulatory bodies have not always taken this view, naturally preferring to have fewer organisations to monitor, but even they in recent years have seemed to recognise that 'small can sometimes be beautiful' even in the voluntary housing movement.

So Cedarmore has remained independent and largely voluntarily managed for this long period. That management may not have been perfect but on the whole it has worked remarkably well, enabling it to develop and administer successfully the projects described in this story.

PART V11
REFLECTIONS

Chapter 27
Today

This book has been written during the latter half of 2008 as we are approaching the 40th anniversary of the formation of Cedarmore as a housing association, following the initiatives described in our first chapter. There was a vision then but it was a relatively simple one and almost certainly none of those involved foresaw its leading to an organisation even as large and demanding as it is to-day. As might be expected, that vision developed as new situations arose and opportunities were embraced. Yet, compared with not a few of the organisations seeking to respond to housing and elderly care needs which had their origins in around the same time, Cedarmore's expansion has been quite limited. Quite a number of the housing associations then formed have since become large very professionally run concerns with central and regional offices, led by directors or chief executives with salaries, some in six figures. Some have taken over responsibilities previously exercised by Local Authority housing departments. Inevitably much of the original vision and some of the altruistic motivation which led to their creation has been lost in the process. Other associations, as we observed in the preceding chapter, have disappeared as they have merged with or been taken over by larger ones. Undoubtedly something has been lost in this process, even though their administrative efficiency and development capacity may well have expanded.

There never has been any desire on the part of those involved in the work of Cedarmore for it to expand into a much larger organisation serving a wider field or need or indeed, as we have observed, to become part of one. It has always only sought to provide a service and meet needs amongst elderly people in the local area and to do this on behalf of local faith communities. The significant expansion which has taken place has been within that framework. A question now to be addressed is as to whether, after even this limited expansion and the greater administrative demands arising from it and in the much changed climate of the 21st century, the organisation and its sheltered and residential schemes conform to the spirit of that original vision. Do they still represent an effective form of Christian service and provide a ministry that meets the need of a small but not insignificant number of elderly people in the area? To answer this question we should perhaps look briefly at each of the schemes as they appear now to be operating.

Cedarmore Court which was opened in 1973 is still operating effectively as a Category I sheltered scheme providing security and support for its elderly residents in its pleasant environment, as described in chapter 3. It remains a very friendly community and, although its design may make it more suitable for more active older people, its residents still seem keen to remain there for as long as possible and 24/7 support is still being provided. There was a recent celebration as one much-loved resident reached both her 90th birthday and her 21$^{st \ year}$ as a resident. She wrote expressing her gratitude for having been offered a place at Cedarmore Court in 1976, saying that her acceptance of it was one of the best decisions of her life! One feature of Cedarmore Court in recent years has been the greater involvement of residents in decisions affecting the amenities of the scheme. This has been encouraged and I gather that some have been surprised to discover how articulate some older people can be. The scheme has good relationships with nearby St Nicholas' Church and Chislehurst Methodist Church, a number of the present residents now attending those churches. One of the problems still appears to be illicit parking by visitors to the neighbouring Bull's Head Hotel. After 35 years, no satisfactory solution to this problem has yet been found! Notwithstanding the attractiveness of this scheme and its pleasant location, and unlike the situation in its early days, local folk do not appear to be rushing to have their names on the waiting list. One reason for this seems to be the unpopularity of bed sitter flats. This is understandable but it is surprising how readily those who do move in seem to be able to adapt to that accommodation and soon find that disadvantage well outweighed by the conducive atmosphere of the scheme and the benefits arising from it.

Southmore Court is still the vibrant community described in chapter 7 where the facilities for residents coming together for meals, parties and social occasions are still being put to maximum use. These activities in which most residents seem happy to participate have added to the sense of mutual care and belonging which the project provides. Outings, even a holiday together for some, seem to be part of the routine. The level of resident satisfaction appears to be very high One of the newer residents, a widower in his eighties who was having great difficulty in coping with life after losing his life long partner, has spoken freely of how living at Southmore has transformed his life. The support of the local church remains strong. And, as at Cedarmore Court, the scheme is blessed with a committed and caring scheme manager and a deputy who do not flinch from going the extra mile when the need arises. And, as at Cedarmore also, there is still a house committee of voluntary helpers which meets three or four times a year to support the manager and keep an eye on the general welfare of residents - a committee of which Douglas has now been the secretary for nearly thirty years! The demand for places there remains high even though much of the accommodation is still in bed sitter flats. This may reflect the sense of community and security when all flats and communal facilities are within the one enclosed block and does seem to correspond with the needs of many elderly people who find it difficult to cope in their present accommodation but are not yet ready for residential care and still want to retain a degree of independence.

Elenmore Court, the newest of the sheltered schemes remains the desirable residence and friendly community described in Chapter 21, at present accommodating four married couples and four residents now on their own. The daily visits from Barbara and others and the close link to Beechmore continue to be a vital part of the shelter provided and one or two of the residents would find it difficult to cope in this accommodation without that support. Tea parties in the conservatory and the occasional outing still seem to be part of Barbara's agenda. Recently, a very elderly couple, both of whose health had deteriorated to the extent that they could no longer manage living in their flat even with domiciliary care visits, were able to move into Beechmore Court and are now being cared for there. Being able to move into the reasonably familiar and neighbouring Home in that situation made the transfer so much easier and more acceptable.

Describing the present situation at Beechmore Court could take much longer. Undoubtedly and not surprisingly, for the management this remains the most demanding of the Cedarmore projects. Those demands fall heavily on the shoulders of the very able and committed Head of Home and on the capable and committed staff team which she has around her as well as on the management committee member chairing the residential care committee who gives so much time to this work. Those demands have not become any less as the proportion of very frail residents and the average age seem to have increased and the paper work and administrative responsibilities seem to have grown. Yet most residents and visitors still see Beechmore as a happy and welcoming place where residents are content and well cared for. If asked, nearly all the Brooker residents would say that they are glad to be there even though they may regret that their age and infirmity have made it necessary. This is undoubtedly because they feel secure and well looked after in this environment. Most relatives of residents, too, seem pleased with the care which their loved one is receiving. One elderly man who is coping in his own home with care visitors four times a day, after staying at Beechmore for one week's 'respite care', liked it so much that he immediately afterwards asked if he could come in permanently. Even more convincing, perhaps, is the comment by John, a highly intelligent bachelor who shortly before his death last year at the age of 97 said that his last seven years as a resident at Beechmore had been amongst the happiest of his life! It is encouraging, too, to see a remarkable change in the appearance of some residents after just a few weeks in the Home - a change which has not gone unnoticed by their visiting friends or relatives.

True, the picture given in Chapter 16 of Beechmore during its early 'golden years' where there was not a single loss of resident during a whole two year period and when there seemed to be a constant round of activities and outings, even staff and residents going on holiday together, could not be repeated to-day. There are activities and occasional outings but, due to their age and frailty, the number of residents willing, and able, to participate in these are less and staff seem to have less time available to give to them. Fortunately, for those who do like activity, there are still volunteers ready to help. Perhaps, with a majority of the residents over 90, some a good deal older and three over 100, it is not surprising that quite a few have little energy for much more demanding activity than reading the paper, listening to the radio or watching the screen.

But the tender loving care for residents which was so much a feature of the Beechmore scene during the time of Ann's, and later Margaret's, leadership remains the same under Julia and is often spoken of by friends and relatives. This is so even though the background of the care staff has changed significantly. In its early days many of the care staff were local residents some of whom had had nursing or caring experience. Nearly all were white. Today, more than half of the carers are from an African or Asian background but the quality and commitment of their care is no less. One very elderly male resident recently told his black middle-aged carer how much he loved her for the tender care which she gave to him! What would care homes and hospitals do were these lovely people from the ethnic minority population not available and willing to do this, sometime unattractive and not too well paid, work for us?

Further evidence of this continuing care is perhaps that nearly all residents who have died during recent years had been able to stay at Beechmore and be looked after there until the end of their lives. Only a small minority have been moved on to nursing homecare or even died in hospital. This is in line with Beechmore's original policy and undoubtedly the wish of most residents but it can place burdens on the care and supervisory staff at the time. It speaks much for the staff that they have always wanted to give such terminal care for one of their residents when needed.

The spiritual side of Beechmore and the distinctive Christian atmosphere of the home is not being overlooked. The regular Sunday afternoon services are well attended by residents, and sometimes their visitors too, and local clergy and lay preachers have been willing to come and conduct these. Visits by the chaplain, Peter, an active retired minister living locally, seem to be appreciated. As well as conducting the services frequently and holding a monthly Communion service, he looks in regularly and ministers to individual needs when called upon. Hopefully, though, the Christian atmosphere of the home is reflected as much in the love and care provided as in its distinctly religious activities.

The work in Florence House and Isabel in the care of residents suffering from Alzheimer's disease or other forms of dementia seems to continue unabated. Quite a few of the present residents have been there for several years. It is demanding work which the staff seems to handle with great patience and understanding, quite a few of the residents being wholly dependant upon the staff for almost every activity.

As expected, the demand for places in the two dementia units seems to be greater than for those in the 'Brooker' section, reflecting the still growing incidence of dementia in older people, particularly as they live longer. It also is a recognition that care in their own homes is not a satisfactory alternative for all dementia sufferers.

In recent weeks this problem has even reached Ambridge where Jack Woolley is now suffering from Alzheimer's disease and his devoted wife Peggy is struggling to care for him. As usual, the Archers' script writers have done their research and portray Jack's conduct in a way typical of those who are in the early stages of this illness. Unfortunately, Peggy herself has had a stroke and has had to go into hospital for several weeks. Her two daughters agree to look after Jack whilst their mother is in hospital but, finding this extremely difficult as Jack cannot come to terms with Peggy's absence, they obtain a temporary place for him in a care home, where he appears to have been looked after well. However, when Peggy returns home after recovering from the stroke, she is very cross with her daughters for having let her down by 'putting him in a home' and immediately takes Jack home and vows to look after him herself. Jack is unable to understand what has happened to Peggy and she assures him that she will never let him go into 'that place' again. The story so far illustrates the sense of failure which many feel if they are no longer able to look after a partner or parent suffering from dementia and have to contemplate placing them in residential or nursing care. If it is true to life, as that programme usually is, Peggy will eventually find that as both her own health and Jack's dementia deteriorate, she will have little alternative but to do so. Seeing how she copes with this will perhaps be as interesting as how Jack settles in the home. Let us hope that there is a Florence House or Isabel or something similar in Borchester or elsewhere near at hand!

And is the voluntary management of the Association still working satisfactorily? From all accounts, it is. The committee structure remains intact and meetings are still being held regularly and proceedings recorded. The Coordinator and Secretary roles are proving vital in ensuring that procedures and regulations are being adhered to and management committee are kept aware of all activities and any problems. The successor to Reg Shore as Chairman of the management committee is another man with considerable business experience, boundless energy and strong Christian commitment and Cedarmore is again blessed in this way.

As might be expected, it is a quite a different management committee to-day than it was even 10 years ago. Hardly any of those who were on the committee during the development years prior to 1998 are still there, several having retired on reaching the age of 80. But other able men and women have come along to share in the management responsibility and several have taken on specific roles which can be time consuming. It is not easy to find the right people to carry such responsibility and Cedarmore appears to have again been favoured in that way.

The finances remain sound as the latest Accounts show although still challenging. The issues discussed in chapter 25 remain part of the financial situation and have to be constantly kept in mind - balancing the need for sound financial management with the desire to provide a high standard of service at a cost affordable to residents.

The support of some of the local churches for the work continues and many of the voluntary helpers and not a few staff and residents come from those communities - as do many of those who organise or attend the Summer and Christmas Fayres which remain popular social and fund-raising events. Even so, with the many good causes looking to

Church congregations for support these days, it sometimes seems easy for them to forget that Cedarmore is a work which has sprung from them and is still dependant on their help and prayers if it is to continue to prosper.

So can we answer the question raised in the second paragraph of this chapter in the affirmative? The unqualified answer must be that we can. Of course, none of the schemes nor the administration are perfect. It is not difficult to find shortcomings if one looks closely enough. But during these past 40 years over 200 people have spent much of their retirement years in one of the three Cedarmore sheltered schemes and a similar number have been cared for in the last few years of their lives at Beechmore Court - and most have been pleased with what they have received. With this record alone it is not difficult to feel that earlier aspirations have been fulfilled and that the work has indeed been blessed. Looking at the work as it now continues, few would not conclude that it is still today an effective ministry and a Christian service which has not departed far from the spirit of that original vision and concept.

And can this be maintained, and perhaps developed further, amidst all the changes and new aspirations of the 21st century? This brings us to our final chapter.

Chapter 28
And Tomorrow?

Much has changed since Cedarmore was started in 1968 and even since Beechmore was opened in 1986 - in both the needs and the expectations of older people themselves as well as in ways of meeting these.   Important changes have taken place also in the statutory and regulatory framework under which such needs can be met.   Over that period too, the number of elderly people in the community needing some support in old age has increased considerably, not least because we are living longer.   Most of their needs are the same in every generation - security, comfort, companionship, to be treated with dignity, to be given as much independence as possible   - and just tender loving care.   Thankfully, our society as a whole is not uncaring and much time and thought, and indeed resources, are being expended in seeking to supply those needs as they arise - and in ways suitable to individual circumstances.   It is worth reflecting for a while on those alternative ways as they are available in our society in 2008. .

It seems to be widely assumed that most older people to-day, even after losing a life-long companion, wish to stay in the family home for as long as possible - almost to the end of their lives - rather than move into some kind of caring environment.   Many find it difficult to face the trauma and upheaval of a move, even into smaller accommodation, and dread the idea of leaving their familiar surroundings for some kind of institutional care.   Social Services Care Managers and other professionals tend to share this assumption. This is not just because it is deemed to be the cheaper option   - they rightly attach importance to the person's wishes.   They, and other agencies, help to make this 'staying put' possible by taking care to that person at home, and seeing that meals are brought to them, rather than encouraging a move into a caring community.   Such help is a life-line in many situations.

However, on closer examination, it becomes clear that this assumption is not always how people feel - particularly where loneliness, perhaps following a close bereavement, or insecurity has become a great problem - or where physical frailty has made coping with quite ordinary chores a great struggle. Over the years, it has been interesting to see the remarkable difference a move into a sheltered or residential care environment has made to the general health of some such people - not least when they have found themselves within a community of people who are friendly and share many of their interests and values..

Perhaps for many the obvious alternative to staying in the family home is to move into sheltered housing , three examples of which we have seen in this story. There is no doubt that sheltered housing for elderly people in some kind or another is here to stay. Its phenomenal growth during the last forty years in both the social and private housing sectors has demonstrated its popularity and its ability to meet the requirements of a significant proportion of the elderly population as they reach their less active retirement years. It enables them to live amongst people of the same generation where there is background support for emergencies and some help at hand and yet still the independence of their own personal accommodation.

The private, public and voluntary sector provision of sheltered schemes has expanded considerably in recent years and many have benefited from moving into them. The ability of these schemes to meet the requirements of older people as their health deteriorates and they need more help and supervision depends on the quality of the support available. Not all will have the on site 24/7 degree of support which is in Cedarmore and other schemes or perhaps are blessed with scheme managers who will go the extra mile to help them when there is a need. Nevertheless, personal care and other support can usually be brought in and a transfer into residential or nursing home care can usually be delayed much longer than would have been possible had the person been living alone in their family home.

Indeed, where the help provided in a sheltered scheme can be strengthened through greater care and some meals provision, it seems that transfer to residential care can be delayed even longer. This may amount perhaps to something like the 'very sheltered housing' which we touched on in Chapter 23.   Is it possible that good sheltered housing, combining maximum independence with support tailored to individual needs, could be the kind of provision most acceptable to many elderly people in today's ageing population?   This might also help the public purse as well as mitigate the dwindling of individual's savings.

Yet for many, there will still come a time when full residential care is desirable and necessary, not least for those for whom a move into sheltered accommodation has been left too late. These people will need and want to be in a small caring community where they find security and comfort and freedom from the chores which they can no longer handle as well as relief from the loneliness which has surrounded them. Another situation where residential care can often be a relief is where someone is finding it impossible to carry the burden of caring for a very frail and dependant partner or relative, even with the support of community carers.   As difficult a decision as this may be for the people concerned, if the dependant partner can be cared for in a good residential home, provided that home is not too far away and has an 'open door' policy, this will enable the partner or relative to spend quality time with their loved one, even help a little, knowing that the main caring burden is on others' shoulders.

Where there is Alzheimer's disease or other forms of dementia, the need for full residential care is almost certainly likely to arise eventually. Florence House and Isabel seem to demonstrate that such care need not necessarily be in an EMI nursing home and can be successfully provided in a small residential setting if sufficient   staff are assigned to it..

Residential care is, of course, more expensive than care at home - although the difference in overall cost, particularly where there needs to be several visits each day, is not always as great as is often perceived. Nevertheless, adequately funding residential care can be a problem. At the moment normal fees barely cover the full cost of providing such care and only do so perhaps because care staff pay is not high.   If pay levels rise as they may well do as the demand for carers increases, the cost will become even higher, further adding to the financial challenge.

When a resident is 'self-funding', he will be reluctant to see much of his savings, mostly derived from the sale of his house, dwindling greatly. This has to be accepted but there must be a case for raising the capital threshold, currently around £23,000, beyond which no help towards fees is available from the Authorities.. It seems reasonable that people should be able to pass on just a little of their life savings to their children.

Where the resident is supported by the Local Authority, there is invariably a shortfall, as we have discussed earlier. This is a problem which seems unlikely to go away in the foreseeable future and finding ways of resolving it remains a challenge for all residential care providers.

Providing care for the elderly, of course, involves employment of staff. It is a labour-intensive activity and the availability of adequately trained and qualified staff to provide, organise and supervise such care is of paramount importance. As we have observed, the need for them is likely to grow. There are many capable and caring people, young and older, working and serving in this way and finding it a satisfying vocation but it is not a career which seems to appeal to many school leavers to-day. Much attention to the recruitment and training and welfare of staff is going to be necessary if care providers are to be able to meet all the demands upon them. The low pay level may have to be addressed and perhaps schools and youth groups could be persuaded to present a more attractive image of this work to their pupils!

These factors and the increasing longevity all seem to point to Governments having to set aside a larger slice of the national budget for the care of the elderly in the future, however that care is provided - a message which is unlikely to be welcome at the moment!.

So, what are the particular challenges facing the Cedarmore organisation itself in this situation? Will it be able to continue to minister to the needs of its relatively small number of elderly residents in the very special manner which it seems to have done in different ways over the past 35 years? Will it be able to continue to provide that high standard of care and service for which it has become known and maintain the satisfaction and contentment which seemed to have prevailed amongst most of its residents? Will it even be able to respond to any new opportunities which might arise? We hope and pray that it will do all these but, for those responsible and who have committed themselves to this service, this will be no easy task.

Foremost, perhaps will be the need for there to be sufficient people who share the ethos of the organisation and have the necessary experience and administrative skills and who are prepared to commit time and energy to share in this responsibility. These are the people who will sit on the management committee and/or one of the subcommittees, with some prepared to take on specific responsibilities. Hopefully, there will be those, perhaps in early retirement, who will catch the vision and want to face this challenge and be prepared to serve in this way for a number of years, particularly when some of the present leaders have to retire. .

Secondly, of course, will be the need to find and retain able, committed and caring staff to continue the work when some of the existing staff leave or retire. As we have seen, Cedarmore has been remarkably provided for in this way over the years through staff who have shared the vision and the objectives. It will be important to replace such people when they have to leave with others who are like-minded and similarly gifted   - and this will not be easy.

Of vital importance to the continuation of the work is the retention of the close links with local churches and their support for this work. As we have seen, the Cedarmore organisation has its roots in a local church and most of those responsible for the work and many of the voluntary helpers have been people associated with one of these   The motivation for the work has always been the desire to exercise concern and care for the welfare of older people as a practical expression of the Christian faith.   Close links to local churches helps to sustain that motivation and their practical and prayerful support is essential.

Coping with the administrative work and bureaucracy surrounding both residential care and sheltered housing and indeed the employment of staff and volunteers and keeping up to date with changes in regulations and guidelines is unlikely to become easier - probably the reverse. Some of this can become very irksome to voluntary helpers who expect their assistance to be people rather than paper-related - but it is important to have some in the organisation willing to master procedures and regulations if trouble is be avoided.

Balancing the books and maintaining financial stability will remain a challenge as pressures both to contain expenditure and limit charges continue. Good financial management will continue to be vital to safeguard such stability and to ensure that the organisation continues to help people in need, irrespective of their financial resources. Charitable funding to meet various needs is still likely to be necessary and good standing in local and church communities is an important factor in this.

And will it be possible still to maintain the independence of such an organisation? As we have observed, of the many small housing associations formed in the 1960's and 1970's, Cedarmore appears to be one of the few that have not since been absorbed into a larger organisation. Others, presumably, felt that their separate mission had been accomplished or were unable to find successors to those who had initiated their work. In most cases, something has been lost through such absorption - often, the local link. The picture of Cedarmore work given in this book may perhaps explain why it has been able to remain an independent local body for so long. Those responsible for the work to-day appear to wish it to continue that way. Its residents and supporters are likely to want this too and I guess that few who look at the quality of its work would think otherwise. It should be able to do this for many years if the people needed become available and the local support for the work continues.

Should that independence ever become impossible, or should for administrative reasons, some close link with another organisation be considered necessary, one hopes that that link would be with an organisation which shares the same ethos, objectives and motivations and would allow the work to remain close to the local community and the local churches.

So the challenges facing the present and future leaders of this work are not small ones and will call for no little commitment and wisdom on their part and some courage. Whatever the future may hold and whatever structural changes may become necessary, one sincerely hopes that the projects which are helping the Cedarmore residents to-day, perhaps changed in some ways to meet changing circumstances, will still be there to serve their successors tomorrow. And there may even be one or two new projects to join them.

May God bless this work in the future as He has so blessed it to this day.

Above
The Front of
Cedarmore Court

Left
The Rear Gardens
of Cedarmore
Court

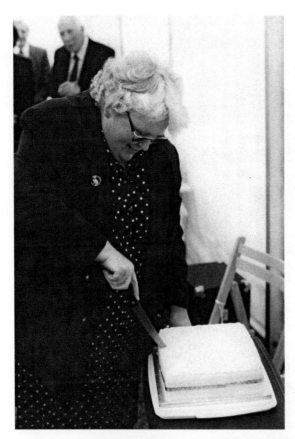

Left
Mary Harding cuts
the cake at Cedarmore
Court's 25th Anniversary

Below
The Front of Southmore
Court

Left
The Rear Gardens of
Southmore Court

Below
The Opening of South-
more Court Heather
presents flowers to Lorna

Above The Front of Beechmore Court
Below The Sun Lounge and Rear Gardens of Beechmore Court

Above The Staff Pantomime at Beechmore Court
Below Beechmore Residents on an outing at Eastbourne

Above Florence House as Built
Below Eileen Cary meets residents of Florence House

Above Elenmore Court as Completed
Below Ron and Iris in their new flat on Opening Day

Above A Special Visitor to Beechmore Court
Below Florence Wakefield

Lightning Source UK Ltd.
Milton Keynes UK
29 October 2009

145542UK00002B/1/P